NO LONGER MISSING!

COMPELLING TRUE STORIES FROM THE SALVATION ARMY'S MISSING PERSONS MINISTRY

Compiled by Judith Brown and Christine Poff

Copyright © 2009 by The Salvation Army

Published by Crest Books
The Salvation Army National Headquarters
615 Slaters Lane, Alexandria, VA 22313

Major Ed Forster, Editor-in-Chief and National Literary Secretary
Major M. Christine Poff, Assistant to the Editor-in-Chief
Judith L. Brown, Crest Books Coordinator

Phone: 703/684-5523
Fax: 703/302-8617

Available from The Salvation Army Supplies and Purchasing Departments
    Des Plaines, IL – (847) 937-8896
    West Nyack, NY – (888) 488-4882
    Atlanta, GA – (800) 786-7372
    Long Beach, CA – (847) 937-8896

Printed in the United States of America

Library of Congress Control Number: 2009922212
ISBN: 9780979226656

Cover photo by Walter Kale, courtesy of the Chicago Tribune
Cover design by Henry Cao
Interior design by Lisa Jones

Contents

Short Stories And Thank–Yous

Acknowledgments

We are grateful to Salvation Army officers and staff who took time away from their busy schedule to help us gather together a diverse collection of rich stories. Without their generous donation of resources, this book would not have been possible.

Major Geoffrey Allan, Chicago, IL
Major Betty Anderson, West Nyack, NY
Major Ruth Miller, Myrtle Beach, SC
Major Douglas Peacock, Long Beach, CA
Major Leslie Peacock, Long Beach, CA
Debra Lewis, Milwaukee, WI
Ken Ramstead, Toronto, Canada

Colonel Jørn Lauridsen, Copenhagen, Denmark
Lt. Colonel Bramwell Pratt, London, England
Lt. Colonel Richard Williams, London, England
Major Nigel Bovey, London, England
Major Colin Fairclough, London, England
Major Laurie Robertson, Victoria, Australia
Family Tracing Services of Australia, Canada, Denmark,
South Africa, Switzerland, and the United Kingdom

Our appreciation is also extended to all of the writers, photographers and other contributors to this book.

Introduction

Finding missing persons is one of the oldest social services offered by The Salvation Army. As early as 1882, The *War Cry* ran its first missing persons notice for a 15–year–old boy named Harry Stout, who was living in northern England. Harry's decision to attend Salvation Army services enraged his father so much that he threatened to break Harry's neck, and the frightened boy ran away. Within a month of the *War Cry* notice, he was spotted in a Sussex village and returned home.

By 1885, the Army had launched an Inquiry Department under Commissioner Florence Booth, the leader of a rapidly growing Women's Social Work Department. As the department flourished, branch offices began to spring up in New York, Chicago, Toronto, Melbourne and Sydney, and an international outreach effort quickly took hold.

America Answers The Call

Around the same time that the missing persons ministry was blossoming in Britain, a large wave of immigrants began to leave overcrowded Europe bound for the United States, Canada, and Australia. Young adults left behind aging parents, brothers said goodbye to sisters, and husbands and wives often stayed separated until they could save enough money to reunite.

The Army's first missing persons office in the United States, known as the Inquiry and Investigation Bureau, opened in New York City in 1910. In 1948, it was renamed the Missing Persons and Inquiry Bureau. Over the years, thousands of clients world-wide have benefited from a service that reflects genuine compassion and concern for their well–being.

In March 2009, resources and strategy for the missing persons program highlighted the agenda of an international social services conference held in Chicago. In 2010, the Army will celebrate the 125th anniversary of this vital ministry.

Starting A Search

> *The mission of The Salvation Army's missing persons program is to reunite people in families who wish to find each other, and to offer supportive guidance, search assistance and spiritual support to those involved.*

To initiate a Salvation Army search, an inquirer first submits a form with a small fee subject to affordability. The following information must be provided to conduct a search:

- Missing person's complete name (including maiden name if a woman)
- Date of birth
- Place of birth
- Parents' names (including mother's maiden name)
- Reason for separation
- Date of last contact
- Inquirer's relationship to missing person
- Reason for the inquiry

The Army generally will **not** pursue a search under the following conditions:

- Individuals seeking friends, i.e., not family members. Cases involving debt collection, child support, or alimony
- Missing and runaway minors, i.e., under 18 years of age, or searches requested by minors

- Children born outside of marriage seeking their natural parent (s), or said parent (s) seeking their children
- Inquiries concerning an estate settlement, a divorce or any other legal matter
- Cases involving custody disputes or "paternal kidnappings"
- Individuals missing less than six months
- Genealogical searches

If the Army decides not to pursue a case, an appropriate referral will be offered. While solving a case can take as little as a week, or as long as a year or more, the use of cutting edge technology has brought about faster and more effective searches. Prayerful support from trained counselors and a respect for confidentiality set the Army apart from information brokers whose skills are not always pastoral.

Essence Of The Program

Faithful workers who carry out the daily essentials of the program insist that they have the best jobs in The Salvation Army. For them, no work is more rewarding or more appreciated than by those who are reunited. Of course, not everyone is found and not every case has a happy ending. Some people may be escaping from a bad environment or an unhealthy relationship, and they may not want to be found.

The initial happy reunion marks only the first step away from hurt and anger toward forgiveness and reconciliation. Relationships demand an ongoing commitment of time and energy, but those who persevere in this worthwhile journey can reap the benefits of transforming grace.

Throughout this book you will encounter compelling stories of people who have been separated for a number of reasons—family tensions, economic problems, mobility, aging and war, to name a few. Although the causes of estrangement may vary, the people involved share a genuine desire to reconnect with a lost loved one. Many of them have lived apart from their families for much of their lives. It takes real courage to reconcile with someone who, even though a blood relative, remains essentially a stranger. The willingness to start anew is a palpable sign that human relationships are holy, second only to our relationship with God.

To initiate a Salvation Army search, contact Major Betty Anderson in the East, 800/315-7699, Betty_Anderson@use.salvation army.org, 440 West Nyack Rd., West Nyack, NY 10994. In the West, contact Major Douglas Peacock, 800/698-7728, Douglas_Peacock@ usw.salvationarmy.org., 180 E. Ocean Boulevard, Long Beach, CA 90802.

Face To Face

Reported by Laurie Goering and Dorothy Post

M ary Ann and her identical twin sister, Susan, had been separated as infants. Susan, of Northfield, IL, and Mary Ann, of Bellevue, WA, were born in Cook County Hospital in Chicago. Their mother had been hospitalized with emotional problems, and their father, unable to care for them, gave them up for adoption when they were just three months old. When the girls were born, adoption agencies had a policy of separating twins, even though both sets of foster parents had wanted to keep the girls together. An overzealous judge used the power of his office to make the separation final and complete. New birth certificates issued at the time of the adoption replaced the names of the biological parents with those of the adoptive parents and omitted any mention of a twin sister.

It must have been the judge's warnings that convinced Susan's adoptive mother not to search for her daughter's twin. Susan, who learned about her twin from her foster mother, honored her mother's wishes by not pursuing a search, but that didn't change her feelings. "I always wanted to find her," she recalls. "I had that urge to know, even as a child."

After Susan's adoptive mother died, she shared her dream of finding her sister with her adoptive father. He responded enthusiastically. "Go for it," he said. Susan's minister at the time was equally supportive and insistent. "You've got to do this," he said.

She spent 10 years trying to find her sister on her own, without success. Finally she turned to The Salvation Army for help, and a month later the Army asked the Social Security Administration to forward a letter to Mary Ann in Washington.

"I thought it was just another advertisement," said Mary Ann. "I opened it, and I was ready to throw it out, but it turned out that there was a letter from Social Security. Then I opened that letter and found another letter from The Salvation Army.

"*Who wants to contact me?*" she asked when she called the Army's Missing Persons Bureau. She knew she had been adopted but had no idea that she had a sibling, let alone a twin. The judge had told Mary Ann's adoptive father that if he tried to find the other twin, he would lose Mary Ann. The family had even been instructed to keep Susan's existence a secret.

So when the answer came back, "Your twin sister wants to contact you," she was flabbergasted.

The Phone Call

At that point, the judge's ultimatums no longer mattered, and moments later, Mary Ann dialed her sister's phone number. Their first conversation in 34 years was lively and emotional, but Mary Ann remembers few words actually being said over the phone that day. "We cried," she recalled. But we didn't get much other stuff in."

With or without words, phone conversations were not enough. A week later Susan was staring anxiously at the arrival gate at O'Hare Airport in Chicago, along with a group of Salvation Army officers, news reporters, and photographers who were on hand to capture the moment.

When the twins finally met face-to-face, they made yet another discovery. Not only were they twins, they were also identical! Describing her first glimpse of her sister, Susan said, "It was like watching yourself get off an airplane!"

She and Mary Ann, both fair-haired and five feet tall, quickly discovered a myriad of likenesses—their voices sounded the same, both had been divorced, both attended church faithfully, and both had poor eyesight. They also shared similar tastes in music, books, movies, and friends. Their favorite color was pink. Their choice of dissimilar occupations, however, set them apart—Susan worked in an office while Mary Ann assembled electronic equipment.

Susan Moves To Washington

The reunion of the twins attracted considerable media attention. "It was reported in newspapers in Washington, Chicago, and all over, I think," said Mary Ann.

Susan made a visit to see Mary Ann in Washington. As she was preparing to return home to Illinois, their story was again recounted, this time on a local radio station. It caught the attention of the owner of a travel agency, the father of twin sons, who offered Susan an airline ticket to relocate to Washington permanently.

Although Susan had been working in Illinois, she felt grateful that her employers encouraged the move. "They said, 'No, you've got to go. You two belong together.'" So the reunion continued—and continues today, many years later.

Since finding each other, Susan and Mary Ann have inherited an enlarged circle of relatives. When Susan first moved to Washington, Mary Ann's daughter Janine was 14 years old. The two women became an integral part of her daily life. "She knew which one was me, but most people can't tell us apart," said Mary Ann. "When Janine was in high school and she brought her friends home, her favorite question to them was 'Which one is my real mom?'"

> Mary Ann had no idea that she had a sibling, let alone a twin.

Susan is especially glad that her adoptive father had a chance to meet Mary Ann before he died. "He loved it," she recalls. "He was so happy that the two of us were together."

Both women agree that their shared life is a good one. Susan values the completeness she experiences. "I don't have that hole, that void, that I always had, that I didn't know how to fill."

Twin sisters, together after 34 years

Laurie Goering's story appeared in the Chicago Tribune. *The story by Dorothy Post, a freelance author and Salvationist, appeared in the* War Cry. *The* Tribune *cover photo is by Walter Kale.*

The Park Bench

Reported by Richard Williams

S ix months of intensive searching by The Salvation Army brought no news of Bill, who had been missing for 13 years.

Sarah, embittered by years of constant fights and bickering, found relief in the relative peace of his absence. Only when their three children had left home did she begin to wonder what had happened to her husband. She had mellowed with the passage of time.

The Army painstakingly traced every scrap of personal information without producing a single lead. Eventually, Sarah learned that all avenues of inquiry had been explored and that the case would be closed. But she was unwilling to take no for an answer.

Although her first *War Cry* posting produced no replies, as a last resort she asked the Army to place a second one. Bill had always brought a copy of the magazine home from the pub on Saturday nights. There was still a chance that he would see the notice.

The Sighting

Immediately after she left the Army's inquiry office, a shocked Sarah reappeared, her face deathly white, her hands clutching her handbag and trembling with agitation.

"I've seen him! I've seen him!" she cried. "Considering it's been 13 years since I last laid eyes on him, I'm still sure it's my husband. He's sitting on a bench across the street."

Peering through the office window, the Salvation Army officer saw an elderly man sitting alone, lifelessly watching pigeons strut at his feet. After looking intently at Bill's picture, he walked over to the park and sat beside him on the bench, pretending to enjoy the sunshine. On scrutinizing his face carefully, there was no doubt it was Bill. This was the man the Army had been searching for all over London.

"Excuse me," the officer said, "are you Bill?" The man turned with a startled expression.

Noting the penetrating eyes and the official uniform, he said, "Yes, that's my name. What do you want?"

Diplomacy

It was not the first time the Salvationist had been asked that question, so his answer had a touch of diplomacy. "Well, it's your family – they're asking about you. We've been looking for you for a long time."

"If it's my wife, I don't want to see her," Bill said emphatically. "But how are the children? What are they doing now?"

"Your youngest son is with the military in Germany. Your other boy is in Coventry, England. Your daughter is married and has two lovely children."

Wheezing with bronchitis, the old man sat for a moment deep in thought. Then he turned and remarked wistfully: "I'd like to see my daughter."

"Okay. Where do you live?"

Immediately Bill was on guard. "Down the road," he replied elusively.

"Which road?" pressed the officer.

Reluctantly, the answer came out, "Victoria Road."

"If your daughter is to come and visit you, I must know the number. You know, we are your friends."

"All right, fair's fair. I have a room at number 37. I'll be there on Thursday afternoon. Ask her to come then."

Bill then lapsed into uncertain, restless thought, until, rising with difficulty, he ambled off. He might have been even less communicative had he known his wife was only 100 yards away.

"It was your husband," the officer told Sarah. "It seems his first thought is for your daughter. He'd like to see her on Thursday afternoon. Your husband looks like a sick man. If he ever comes home, I think he would need a lot of care."

The next morning, as the officer approached his office building, his associate called to him urgently from the entrance.

"Come quickly. Bill's daughter is on the phone."

Tired Of Waiting

Barbara, eager to see her father, could not wait until Thursday. Could she come at once? Glancing across the road, the officer told her that her father was, at that moment, sitting on the bench. "Yes, certainly. We'll make sure he doesn't wander away before you get here."

Within an hour a very excited Barbara arrived.

Returning to the park bench, the officer told Bill, "Your daughter is in my office. She's here to see you."

Bill didn't need to be asked twice. His shaky legs couldn't carry him fast enough. When Barbara saw her father she immediately embraced him and smothered his emaciated, unshaven face with kisses. The officer quickly left the office to avoid intruding on this intimate reunion.

> "Yes, that's my name. What do you want with me?"

Half an hour later when he brought them some refreshments, their faces were glowing.

"I'm taking him home to see Mom," said Barbara. "We're going right now."

The officer thought that the case was closed, but it wasn't. The following morning, again on his way to work, and preoccupied with new problems, he failed to notice an elderly couple walking arm-in-arm down the street. They called to him. It was Bill and Sarah, both looking delighted.

A few minutes later, from his office window, he saw them sitting together on Bill's bench. Even the pigeons seemed to strut more lightly and to preen more contentedly. Barbara, camera in hand, joined her parents. She recorded this scarcely believable occasion with a photo.

The Salvation Army officer was called over to join in the photo. At first he thought the old couple was inviting him to sit between them. But Sarah dug her thin, sharp elbow into him.

"No, Captain, you can't sit there. You come and sit on this side. Bill and I've been separated long enough."

A New Home

A couple of weeks passed before the reunion was complete. Sarah was living in a second floor apartment, and Bill could not climb the stairs because of heart trouble and bronchitis. The landlord quickly arranged a housing exchange for them, and the next day they moved into a ground floor apartment. Now the captain knew for certain that the Army's role in the story had reached an end.

This story appeared in Lt. Colonel Richard Williams' book, Missing! The Inside Story of the Salvation Army's Missing Persons Departments. *He served as head of the Family Services and Inquiry Department in London.*

A Lawyer Goes Undercover

Reported by Linda Johnson and Ruth Miller

J ennifer was suspicious when she received a letter from the Social Security Administration saying that her mother was searching for her. She felt sure that the couple who had raised her were her biological parents, and her birth certificate carried both their names.

The Conversation

Curious, and confident that her privacy would be protected, Jennifer answered the inquiry and a few weeks later she received the name, address, and telephone number of a woman living in Brooklyn. Assuming the woman was either delusional or a fraud, she called and posed as a missing persons investigator.

The woman knew many facts about Jennifer, details that only she and her family could have known. Jennifer kept her composure and continued to ask questions, not revealing her identity yet.

"I don't want to interfere in her life," the unsuspecting birth mother said, "but I wonder if she is all right, if there is anything I can do to help her—I wonder if she ever had any children."

After interviewing the woman for about an hour, Jennifer ended the call, promising to do everything in her power to help her. Convinced of the woman's sincerity, she summoned the courage to confront the only woman she had ever called "Mom."

Her adoptive mother's telephone was busy for hours, and then it finally rang through. She had just returned from the doctor's office after learning that she had probably lost her sight in one eye due to a fall. Jennifer knew it was not a good time, but she had to know. Sometimes her mother had joked that she had been adopted. It was true, wasn't it? "Yes," her mother said simply.

The Whole Truth

The truth came tumbling out. She explained that Jennifer's biological mother had left her suave, unfaithful husband before learning that she was pregnant. Her obstetrician contacted a lawyer friend who was representing a childless couple.

The adoptive parents took the baby home, telling their relatives that Jennifer was their natural child. Then her biological mother decided that she had made a mistake and tried to get her daughter back, but her adoptive parents refused. In court, Jennifer's birth mother agreed to relinquish her parental rights in return for two and one-half years of visitation privileges. She remarried and moved to Brooklyn to be closer to her daughter, who was strikingly beautiful with large blue eyes and blond hair. From a distance she watched the baby to make sure that she was in a good home.

Then, without warning, the adoptive parents left Brooklyn. Jennifer's birth mother tried to track them down using a private investigator, following cold leads as far away as Denver.

For 42 years, she wondered whether her daughter was dead or alive. She and her second husband had two sons, but every year she thought about how old her little girl would be on her birthday. Eventually, she gave up hope of ever finding her.

Meanwhile, Jennifer grew up in Florida, puzzled as to why she had wanted to be a journalist ever since the sixth grade. At the age of 14, she landed her first job as a reporter/photographer on a daily newspaper. Later, she entered law school to become a better journalist but decided to follow a career in law. She was the only person in her extended family to qualify for Mensa, the international organization for people with IQs in the 98th percentile or higher. She asked herself why spiritual growth was such a priority for her, while neither of her parents seemed to care. In her 40's she joined a chorus as a first alto. Where did her love of music come from?

Jennifer redialed the Brooklyn phone number, knowing that she had at least 42 years to make up. After a brief, emotional conversation with her birth mother, she gave the phone to her husband, her nine-year-old son and her seven-year-old daughter. It was discovered through tears that they were her mother's only grandchildren.

Identity Crisis

The call continued for several hours. Many times Jennifer and her mom tried to say goodbye, but a new topic came up and they continued talking, laughing and crying.

Her mother, with a journalism degree from Bennington College, had a brother who was a retired newspaper editor with an IQ of 170. She had sung alto in a choir and had an older sister who had gone to law school.

The conversation lasted all night long.

At six a.m., mother and daughter agreed to count to three and hang up at the same time. The next day Jennifer mailed her mother a priority envelope with photographs, news clippings, a resume and other memorabilia from her life.

> From a distance she watched the baby to make sure that she was in a good home.

It wasn't long, however, before her euphoria spiraled into a free fall. Who was she? Everything she had believed about herself had changed, including medical facts about her family that she had given to her physician. Although she had childhood memories, she had been too young to recall anything about her mother's visits. Supported by counsel from wise friends, she managed to muddle through her depression and regain her emotional equilibrium.

A Mother–Daughter Reunion

Filled with ambivalence, Jennifer flew with her family to New York to attend a reunion with her mother. Her stepbrother came to meet his sister and treated everyone to a Chinese dinner. There was plenty of time to talk and to take photos. After this startling experience, Jennifer was completely convinced that genetics play a key role in who people become, and that children have a right to know they are adopted.

Linda Johnson is the Editor of Priority! *Magazine, a Salvation Army publication. Major Ruth Miller served as the director of The Salvation Army's missing persons office in West Nyack, NY.*

Left For Dead

Reported by Colin Fairclough

I n Fiji, Joan was visibly shaken when she noticed a story in her local newspaper about a trial for an attempted homicide in northern England. This wasn't just any random act of violence. She instantly recognized the victim of this horrific crime as her daughter, Talei, whom she had not seen since Talei was a baby. The family resemblance, however, was undeniable.

The article reported that 17-year-old Talei had met John, a restaurant owner, while on a Christmas cruise with her adoptive parents. Talei married John less than six months later, and later they moved into an apartment above a new restaurant that John had purchased.

A Wicked Scheme

After John's business began to suffer a downturn, he devised a fiendish scheme in order to save himself from bankruptcy. His plan was to kill Talei in order to collect $600,000 in life insurance money. He hired a hit man to carry out the murder, and while he remained in the restaurant, the hired killer attacked Talei in their upstairs living room. She was struck on the head with an iron bar, and her throat was cut so deeply that her windpipe was left exposed. Altogether, she suffered 11 cuts to her skull, a five-inch cut to the front of her neck, fractured ribs and a collapsed lung.

Left for dead in a pool of blood, Talei miraculously survived and recovered to identify her attacker. The police then traced the crime back to her husband and arrested him for attempted murder. Following his trial, John received a prison sentence of 15 years, while the attacker was sentenced to a term of 11 years.

Back in Fiji, Talei's birth parents, Joan and Paul, read the account of the trial occurring in England and recognized her as the daughter they had given up for adoption immediately after her birth. They had been only in their mid-teens when she was born. Meanwhile, Terry and Millie, her adoptive parents—who were also then living and working in Fiji—were delighted to take her into their home. Shortly afterwards, they returned with Talei to their home in England.

Government Intervention

Joan and Paul sought the help of the British Ambassador in Fiji to contact Talei. In turn, the ambassador asked The Salvation Army to offer guidance on this rather sensitive matter. Although it was not the sort of inquiry the Army would normally undertake, exceptional circumstances called for an exceptional response.

> **Certain that the victim was their daughter, the Wilsons sought the help of the British Ambassador.**

The first step was to get documentation from Fiji confirming the details of Talei's birth and adoption. This was quickly sent by fax. Terry and Millie were contacted, and Millie was pleased to learn of the inquiry from Talei's birth parents.

A couple of days later, she called the Army to report that Talei was eager to be in touch with her birth mother. Joan and Millie then spoke on the telephone.

During the media frenzy that followed, Talei, Terry and Millie appeared on a television program to talk about the ordeal. By that time, Talei was in regular contact with her birth family in Fiji.

Years later, Talei wrote to The Salvation Army, describing her 12,000-mile trip from northern England to visit her newly discovered family in Fiji. In addition to her birth parents, she met her grandmother, three uncles, and a host of cousins. The visit lasted seven weeks, and she didn't want to leave. Later she started her own design business and gave it a Fijian name that means, "place in the sun."

Major Colin Fairclough served as director of The Salvation Army's Family Tracing Service in England.

Finally A Family

Reported by The Salvation Army's Chicago Office

W hen people are introduced to Barbara and Rusty for the first time, they are struck by the strong family resemblance. Both have reddish brown hair, similar facial features, kind eyes, and gentle, inviting personalities. They seem genuinely at ease with each other and at peace with the world.

They value simple, unhurried activities like doing dishes, talking, and rocking on the front porch of their old farmhouse. In a video made for The Salvation Army, one scene shows 10 relatives gathered at a long, ranch style table sharing a home-cooked meal. This serene, unassuming lifestyle honors the sacredness of ordinary moments and invites the grace of God to permeate all that they say and do. But it hasn't always been that way.

Mother's Illness

Barbara and Rusty belonged to a family of five children born to three different fathers. Barbara recalls that when she was about five years old, their stepfather went to jail, and their mother was left sick and alone. "I remember them taking my mother away in an ambulance and I was just standing there. They grabbed Richard (another brother) as he got off the school bus."

Barbara and Richard were kept together until she was nine and he was 11 years old. After that she lived in five foster homes and two orphanages.

When the family broke up, Rusty was an infant and Evelyn was two years old. Both of them were adopted by a family and eventually moved to New Jersey. Barbara recalls her foster mother taking her to see them before they moved. "Evelyn remembered me, but Rusty was only a baby. I remember a little blond-headed boy running around, but he didn't notice me."

Even though Barbara grew up in foster care, she remained in contact with her mother and Richard. But she was unable to find out what had happened to her other siblings.

A Classified Job

Rusty had joined the Navy Seals and had managed to live his life without leaving a paper trail. Because his work was classified, his identity and privacy were heavily guarded, so any searches for him had turned up empty. Barbara had spent years patiently looking for him on her own, sometimes checking all 50 states on the Internet. Heeding the advice of a friend, she finally turned to The Salvation Army Missing Persons Bureau. The breakthrough in the case came when Rusty and his wife bought and financed a new car. Finally there was a paper trail to follow.

It took The Salvation Army six months to find Rusty. He didn't even know that he and Evelyn were adopted until he received a letter from the Army. Assuming it was a request for a donation, he had tossed it aside without even reading it. By chance, his daughter noticed the opened letter lying on the coffee table and informed him, "Dad, they say you have a missing family member."

"No, I don't," Rusty insisted.

"At first, I thought they were talking about Evelyn looking for me," Rusty said. "She left home on my 16th birthday and I didn't know where she was. But the letter said I had a sister named Barbara, so I didn't have a clue."

Rusty felt a little anxious when he dialed the phone number for Barbara, who, of course, was a total stranger to him. She was not at home when he called, but he ended up talking to his nephew for at least an hour.

When Rusty came to meet Barbara, she picked him up at the airport, and the two siblings recognized each other immediately. They drove to meet their older brother Richard, and they've all been in communication ever since.

Gratitude

Evelyn and their oldest brother, Donald, have been found as well. Evelyn had left her adoptive home to escape an abusive relationship. Rusty remembers the way she used to tenderly care for him when he was a young boy. When she left home, he had to fend for himself, and eventually he decided to join the Navy.

All five of the children are back in touch and working to restore the family relationships that were severed so many years ago. For soft-spoken Barbara, the long-term impact of a broken family has been no less than "devastating."

> He didn't even know that he was adopted until he received a letter from the Army.

Rusty is thrilled and amazed over this remarkable turn of events. "How does someone have that much love . . . that they'd go that long and work that hard to find me? It's wonderful to have this new family all of a sudden. I'm not close to my adoptive family, and I was grateful to have my wife and daughters, but look at me now!"

"I'm grateful to God and the miracle He's given us," says Barbara. "We're going to do whatever it takes to keep our family together now."

Making Sense Of The Past

Reported by Johanna D. Wilson and Ruth Miller

E)ven as an adult, the little girl in Tammy Miller burst forth when she looked into her father's eyes. She was giggly, bold, happy and hopeful because she could reach over and hug her dad, Elwood.

Both attitude and aptitude made their reunion possible after a separation of more than 30 years. And it didn't hurt to have an experienced private investigator in the family.

"This is a dream I never thought would come true, and sometimes I felt like giving up," Tammy said. "But I didn't, and now I'm sitting next to my dad."

Before their reunion at her home in Myrtle Beach, Tammy had not seen her father since she was about six years old, when financial and emotional strain wedged them apart.

"We're doing great now, and we plan on keeping in touch," said her dad. "This is our new beginning. Now I can rest in peace."

A Personal Private Eye

It was Tammy's mother-in-law, a licensed private investigator named Ruth Miller, who finally supplied the balm needed to heal Tammy's wounds.

"Tammy gave me all the information she could remember, and she was doing a lot of searching on the Internet," Ruth said. "I guess my ego got the best of me because I didn't want Tammy to find him before I did. So I picked up the pace."

After about five years of searching, Ruth won the race with her daughter-in-law when she sent a letter to Auburndale, FL, where she thought Elwood was living. He no longer lived there, but an older daughter, Laura, called her father at work to let him know he had received a certified letter from an investigator.

"I hadn't been in South Carolina for years, and I thought, 'Who could be looking for me?'"

After work, he went straight to Laura's house and read the letter. They cried together, and he called Ruth to let her know he was the long sought after father.

"He left a message on my answering machine," said Ruth. He said, "I'm calling to tell you that Tammy is my daughter."

What Happened?

Tammy was still shell-shocked from the events that had split up her family when she was a little girl in Henderson County, NC. She struggled to understand why her family had been dysfunctional. "I had a bad life," she said sadly. "It was rough. I didn't have the best Mom."

Elwood struggled to care for his wife and their six children, but when he lost his job, the family spiraled into dire financial straits. Even a new job in South Carolina wasn't enough to keep his family together.

"I was miserable," he said, "and I was permanently separated from Tammy's mother, who struggled with alcoholism. It wasn't easy, and I have to admit I turned to the bottle, too."

Foster Care

Officials from the Henderson County Department of Social Services eventually placed all of the children in foster care, group homes, and later with adoptive families. Tammy lost touch with all of her siblings except for her younger brother. "He and I made a pact not to be split up because we were the youngest two," she said.

Elwood visited his five older children in the foster homes where they were placed, but he couldn't find Tammy and his youngest son. Both of them had left Henderson County after being adopted by a family living in another part of North Carolina.

Although Tammy's adoptive parents were caring, she rebelled, turning to alcohol and drugs to drown her grief over the loss of her biological family. She had felt disillusioned and unloved.

Rebel With A Cause

"Everything hit me at once, and I started feeling angry," she said. "It was a time bomb, and I exploded. I started partying every night and getting high. My past had caught up with me."

Her adoptive parents kicked her out of the house when she was 18 years old because of her reckless behavior and lack of respect for their rules. She ended up at a friend's house and finally got fed up with herself.

"I got tired of living a wild and crazy life, and I decided I didn't want that life anymore," she said.

After moving to Monroe, SC, Tammy married and then gave birth to a daughter. She managed to earn her G.E.D. and began working in the hotel industry.

> "I got tired of living a wild life, and I decided I didn't want that life anymore."

Finding Dad

When life didn't go well in Monroe, she divorced, then moved to Myrtle Beach, SC, and temporarily gave her daughter to her grandparents. In Myrtle Beach, she met and married Kenny, whose mother, Ruth, now retired from The Salvation Army, was working as a licensed private investigator.

Tammy and Kenny had a son, and she and her daughter were eventually reunited. Ruth was able to locate Tammy's dad, who was a changed man, living in Florida. Elwood, who had since remarried, had already found Tammy's siblings and had spent thousands of dollars trying to find his daughter.

Since reconnecting with her dad, there have been joyous Christmas reunions at Tammy's home. Tammy, Kenny and their son traveled to Florida on a camping trip and stopped at her sister's home to visit their family. They also took a trip to Disney World and spent several days with relatives. Tammy's dad has been able to supply her with important medical information that she had been lacking.

The only family member missing now is Tammy's mom. "I hope to find her," she said. Until then, she's doing fine with her dad. "I feel more satisfied since finding my dad," Tammy said. "I'm happy."

Tammy with her dad, Elwood

Johanna D. Wilson's story appeared in the Sun News, *Myrtle Beach, SC. Major Ruth Miller also contributed to this story. Photos courtesy of Tammy Miller and Ruth Miller.*

A Christmas To Remember

Reported by Colin Fairclough

S ister Marie's father, George, left her in a convent in India when she was only four years old. As an employee for the railroad, he managed to earn enough money to cover the cost of her education. When she was a young child he came to see her often, but at some point the visits ceased. Marie grew up to be a teacher in the convent. She studied in Rome and taught for a while in the United States.

When she received word that her father had died in London, she felt puzzled as to when and why George had moved to England, as well as who had reported the news of his death. The years passed, and when she was almost 60 years old, Marie received permission from the Superior General of her religious order to visit a convent in England. Her leave of absence would give her time to solve the mystery of her father's life and death, and to determine whether she had other living relatives.

A Sister And A Brother

Through The Salvation Army, Marie learned that the person who had contacted the convent was her sister, Gloria, who had since died. Gloria's death certificate revealed that she had also been born in India, and that she had a brother named Eric. But Marie didn't know how to find him until a friend put her in touch with The Salvation Army's Family Tracing Service.

On a pilgrimage to Lourdes, France, Sister Marie prayed for the success of the Army's Family Tracing Service. Eric wrote within a few weeks to confirm that he was the person she was seeking, although he had no idea that he had a younger sister.

Holiday Joy

By then, Marie had been transferred back to Rome. Once again, her superiors gave her permission to visit England to see her new relatives. Eric and his family arranged for her to spend the Christmas holidays with them.

Sister Marie later wrote to The Salvation Army, "For the first time in my life, I shared Christmas with a family. I'm so grateful to God for all the marvels He has done for me, with you as my adviser and guide. I thank you for this miracle of grace. I don't know if I will ever get another chance to see my relatives, but I'm going away with hope and trust in my heart. God is with me—my Good Shepherd—who will lead me into green pastures. I invoke God's blessings on you in a very special way. So with this I end, with a heart full of gratitude."

> "For the first time in my life, I shared Christmas with a family."

Shortly afterwards, Sister Marie was transferred back to a teaching position in India. Her family did not know that she was suffering from cancer.

Marie died a few years later, without seeing her relatives again. Her sister-in-law said that, "in her own words, Marie was ready to go to her heavenly home."

Undeliverable

Reported by The Salvation Army's Chicago Office

J eri, who lived in Norway, wanted to find her older sister Joni. Their mother, in Colorado, had been diagnosed with brain cancer. Jeri's family had not seen or heard from Joni in several years.

The Salvation Army's Missing Persons Bureau in Chicago sent a letter to an address in Texas, which was returned marked "undeliverable." When the letter came back, a caseworker noticed that the Texas address had an addendum that read "Expatriate–Norway." Should the application form have been sent to the office in Norway?

The letter contained no Norwegian address, but it included what seemed to be an international phone number. Although the workday had long since ended, a call was made to Jeri to inquire about her correct mailing address. Unfortunately, the staff didn't realize that it was the middle of the night in Norway. The caseworker apologized for waking Jeri out of a sound sleep, especially since any phone call could bring bad news about her mother. To make matters worse, since she lived in Norway rather than the United States, she would have to re–start her search through the Missing Persons Bureau in her own country.

The Chicago staff, fearing that the mother might die before they could find Joni, decided to waive protocol and pursue the case, anyway. They found Joni's social security number, which revealed that she had moved every six months for the past 14 years. None of the information was current, but for some strange reason, a three–year–old phone number caught one worker's eye. It actually turned out to be the right one.

Joni had been in a difficult marriage, had moved often, and had lost all contact with her family. When the phone rang, she and her new husband were eating dinner and discussing their daughter's striking resemblance to aunt Jeri. For years Joni had tried to find her family by searching the Internet without success. The caseworker told her to call Jeri in Norway right away, despite the late hour.

> For years Joni had tried to find her family, searching the Internet without success.

After learning that her mother was hospitalized in Colorado, Joni and her husband, who lived in Florida, made plans to visit her. She also learned that another sister was living in Florida and that she had a brother in Virginia.

In a follow-up conversation with The Salvation Army, Joni's husband thanked the missing persons staff not only for reuniting the two sisters, but also an entire family—mother, sisters, brother, cousins, nieces and nephews. "It's truly a miracle that you called when you did. Our lives will be forever blessed," he said.

She Never Forgot

Reported by Chris Parker

ixty-five-year-old Mildred stood at the airport gate, nervously rubbing her thumb on the smooth leather of her wallet and craning her neck to view the passengers walking up the ramp. Suddenly her hands stilled. A wide smile crept across her face and tears glistened in her eyes as Geraldine, the sister she hadn't seen since they were toddlers, fell into her arms.

It was the first time the sisters had hugged each other since their mother left with Geraldine and their brother Robert. Mildred and another brother, George, were left behind with their father and his parents on a farm near Philadelphia. Mildred, who lived in Forest Inn, PA, and Geraldine, of Ellensburg, WA, clutched each other's hands as they walked through the airport, chatting all the way.

"I'll bet we held each other's hands like this when we were little, until someone pulled us apart," Mildred said, smiling through tears.

Geraldine couldn't stop grinning. "It's a dream come true," she said. "I'm finally going to have a sister I can say is mine."

The sisters were reunited after an eight-month search by The Salvation Army, which culminated in Mildred finding her sister and brother as well as three half-siblings unknown to her.

The last time she had seen Geraldine, people were flocking to see the comedy, "Bringing Up Baby," starring Cary Grant and Katherine Hepburn. The Baseball Hall of Fame was opening in Cooperstown, NY, and a young broadcaster named Orson Welles was inciting mass hysteria with his dramatization of a Martian invasion, "The War of the Worlds." At the time, the girls were oblivious to movies, baseball and radio broadcasts. All the toddlers knew was that their secure little world had been shattered.

"I think my mother was very, very confused," Mildred said. "My father wouldn't answer any of my questions," she added. "Not even when I was older."

Memories

Mildred's only clue was that her mother had left one day with her brother and sister. Much later she learned that her mother had been pregnant at the time. "All we knew was that she had long blonde hair and was a little on the heavy side," she said. "Now we know why she was heavy—she was expecting a baby."

> All the children knew was that their secure little world had been shattered.

Although Mildred was only three years old when her mother left, she never forgot about her sister and brother. "She's been looking for them all our married life," said her husband Charles. The couple has three grown children.

In an attempt to publicize her search, Mildred unsuccessfully invested hundreds of dollars in books of addresses and contacted television talk show hosts. She also wrote a letter to the Social Security Administration, to no avail.

Discouraged, but not defeated, she decided to contact The Salvation Army. It took eight months to locate Geraldine and her brother Robert of Hanford, CA, as well as half-siblings Mary, of Wenatchee, WA, and Candy and JoAnn, also of Hanford, CA. Another sister, Delores, remains missing. George, a brother who had been left behind with Mildred, had died.

Chris Parker's story appeared in The Morning Call, *Allentown, PA.*

Recovery And Reconciliation

Reported by Richard Seven and Camilla Warrick

F or most of 22 years, Glen's only company was a bottle. But now this resident of a Salvation Army Adult Rehabilitation Center (ARC) in Seattle is back on good terms with his 14 children and 28 grandchildren—thanks largely to a persistent daughter named Aggie.

A recovering alcoholic, Glen had deserted his family in Madison, IN. He left behind all photos, letters and personal attachments and never looked back. He even changed the spelling of his last name.

"I was an alcoholic and a bad one," he said. "I felt it would be better for my kids and everyone if I just got out of their lives." Whiskey didn't kill him, but it did weaken the family finances, botch his employment record, and drain him of hope. So one day he just disappeared.

On The Road

Glen packed a suitcase, climbed into a friend's 18-wheeler and rode as far south as Atlanta. Then he boarded a bus for Florida. By the time he arrived, he had left behind his old name and former responsibilities.

He became a man who could swallow a quart of whiskey and close down the bars in the pre–dawn hours if he wanted to. But he could never go back to his home in Madison, IN. That was his self-imposed sentence. "They'll never forgive me," he'd tell himself. Then he'd try to forget, figuring that's what his family was doing.

But he figured wrong. For 21 years, all of his children kept remembering. Aggie remembered his blue eyes, his brown hair and his nimble hands that could fix any broken engine. Although she never tried to justify her father's leaving, she always said he was a good man—when he wasn't drinking. She kept a snapshot that showed him leaning against a pickup truck, the corners of his mouth curled into a smile, his arms loaded with children. There were 13 of them and a 14th on the way. Glen had never met his son, George, who was born only three weeks after he left home.

Persistence

The children never gave up trying to find their father. They worked through relatives, police departments, utility companies, the Social Security Administration, and Chambers of Commerce. After several attempts, Aggie finally hit pay dirt when she contacted The Salvation Army's Missing Persons Bureau. The Army uncovered Glen's assumed name and a nine-year-old address. The age was right, and so were his height and weight. His hair had not even turned gray, and yes, his hands were still very nimble.

He had been living in Salvation Army shelters, and searchers found him sober at a facility in Seattle. To everyone's amazement, he was on the organization's payroll, working as a maintenance supervisor for a large fleet of trucks. He hadn't tasted a drop of alcohol in more than three years.

Aggie wrote him a letter saying it was time to start over because all of his 14 children wanted to see him again. She stuffed the envelope with notes from each of his sons and daughters explaining why they wanted to find him.

When Glen called a few days later he could barely talk. "I thought all you kids hated me," he told Aggie between sobs. "I thought I'd die without ever seeing you again."

Five of his children went to spend the weekend with him. They stayed in a Salvation Army center and talked day and night. "I feel like I've been reborn," he said, beaming with a wide grin. "This shows that the Man up there never gave up on me."

Glen had worked with a Salvation Army officer for six years in Pasadena and Van Nuys, CA, then finally, Seattle, WA. The officer never knew that Glen had a family. "He was in and out of the ARC program so often in the early days that my staff started saying I wasn't following my own rules," he recalled. "But Glen came back and the transformation has been astounding."

Patriarch

For the first time in his life, 21-year-old son George got to meet his father. "If nothing else, I just wanted to see what he looked like," George said. "I think we were all kind of worried he might get cold feet and not show up."

But Glen was at the airport to greet his children. Because he was afraid that he wouldn't recognize them, he held up a large sign with his name on it. He had disappeared so thoroughly that he didn't know that his parents had died. Even his son Dan, a police officer, had been unable to trace him through the department's computer.

His room at the Salvation Army center overflowed with letters, photos of weddings and of 28 grandchildren he didn't even know he had. Like any proud father, he bragged about his children. They updated him on their friends, their family and their mother, who had remarried and had three more children.

> "I thought all you kids hated me."

'The reunion was better than anyone had dared to hope," Aggie said. "It seemed like we'd known him all our lives."

"I'm one happy person," said Glen. "I've laughed more in the past few days than I have in 22 years. They've all turned out so well, and they don't drink. Maybe everything I went through was worth it."

Now the man who vowed never to go home wants to return to Indiana. He says he's got to see his kids. Maybe he'll stay a month. Or just maybe, forever.

Glen, his daughter Aggie, and other family members

Richard Seven's story appeared in the Seattle Times. *Camilla Warrick also reported this story in her* Seattle Inquirer *column. Photo by Harley Soltes.*

An Appalling Truth

Reported by Bramwell Pratt

E)llen prepared tea and then glanced at the clock. It was 5:55 p.m., and John would be home any moment now. He was rarely early or late.

For about 20 years they had lived quietly in their suburban London home. In their contented domestic routine, life had seemed to go by without anything happening to disturb their lives. After all, they had not met nor married until both were in their forties.

Out Of Character

By 7:00 p.m., John had not made an appearance. Nor at 8:00 or 9:00—this had never happened before. He had said nothing about being late when he left that morning. Now that Ellen thought about it, he had looked a bit pale and strangely tense, although she had not commented on it. She knew he had some concerns about his approaching retirement.

Ellen walked to the pay telephone on the corner and called John's manager, who was surprised to hear from her. Didn't she know that he had given notice at the firm a week ago? They were sorry to lose him because he was so reliable. Everyone thought that he could have waited a few more months until he retired.

Ellen hid the fact that this was shattering news to her. A cold, creeping numbness gripped her. Her mind darted here and there seeking an explanation, but she could find none. She and John had always been so close. It was unbelievable and entirely out of character for him not to come home. Could there possibly be a connection between his absence and the letter he had received from the pensions department a week or two before? He had been unusually quiet, even irritable, since that letter came.

Then Ellen began to connect the dots in her mind. The previous week she had found him going over his clothes, remarking that summer was coming and that they needed to go to the cleaners. When Ellen looked in his closet, it was almost empty and his suitcase was gone.

Tired and anxious, the next morning she went to see if the officials dealing with her husband's pension could throw any light on the matter. She found the government reluctant to give her any information at all.

The police wouldn't even place John on the missing persons list. Wasn't it obvious that her husband had planned to leave? "This is a free country, ma'am," she was told. Baffled and alone with her grief, and with all of her questions unanswered, Ellen struggled to cope with the emotional contradictions that inevitably arose.

When a sympathetic neighbor suggested that The Salvation Army might be able to trace her husband, she traveled to their headquarters in London. Telling her story to the friendly Salvationist who interviewed her, Ellen began to realize how little her husband had revealed to her about his earlier years. She had never inquired too deeply into his past.

After a lengthy conversation with Ellen, the caseworker concluded that John was thoughtful, intelligent and careful— someone who would leave no tracks that might permit anyone to trace him. Inquiries were made in a dozen towns and cities. After a few weeks the Army managed to forward a letter to John. This was the moment that Ellen had hoped for—the chance to tell him that she still loved him and wanted him home with her more than anything. If he was in trouble, they could face it together.

Breaking The Silence

For seven days there was anxious suspense. Then two letters arrived from John, one for his wife, and the other seeking guidance for his dilemma. For more than 20 years he had carried a guilty secret that he feared would emerge through the arrangements for his pension. It wasn't the authorities he feared, or even the consequences of breaking the law, but the hurt Ellen would suffer when she knew the truth.

The name he had used wasn't his after all. It was the name of the pharmacist who had hired him when he was young, after both of his parents had died. He had been on the verge of apprenticeship when his employer died.

His marriage to Ellen had been bigamous. Alone and with little knowledge of life, he met and married his first wife, Agnes, after a brief courtship.

The relationship did not work out well. Perhaps the scars of grief went deeper than he knew. Maybe his introverted personality and a natural reserve created barriers between them. Despite the birth of a son, neither of them was happy.

Deeply depressed, John was at home one evening taking care of the baby, who seemed to cry incessantly. Almost overwhelmed by black rage, he felt tempted to take the baby and throw him to the ground. He knew he had reached the breaking point. Unable to face life, death or even his own identity, John left home. Sometimes he begged enough for a night's lodging in a cheap boarding house. Sometimes he found refuge in a public shelter. Dirt and fleas became his daily lot. His only joy lay in being close to nature.

> Didn't she know that he had given notice at the firm the week before?

Perhaps springtime gave birth to a desire to take hold of life again. He began to do casual work the first few years, and with awakening confidence and ambition he found a good job and eventually settled down. Then he joined the Air Force, began to find himself, and met Ellen.

A New Life

She was petite, pretty, and the sort of person he could talk to easily. They fell deeply in love, decided to marry, and established a quiet, peaceful home life. Even though John tried to erase all memories of his past, he inevitably began to feel contempt for himself. Sometimes he wondered what had happened to Agnes and his son, and whether, after 40 years, she had divorced him or even died. He was afraid to make inquiries that might engender record searches or prompt visits to his old neighborhood. Sooner or later he had to tell Ellen the appalling truth.

In his confusion and solitary unhappiness, his decision to leave home didn't feel cowardly. Haunted for years by his crime of bigamy, he was sure the authorities would discover it when he filed for his pension. The retribution of the law would fall on him, and Ellen would suffer public humiliation.

To leave her would at least preserve her self-respect and give him time to write and tell her the truth. He would send her support and allow the passage of time to ease her pain and erase her affections.

Although Ellen still loved John and wanted to be with him, he continued to live in a distant town while she stayed in their small home, anxiously awaiting the results of an inquiry into their marital status. She decided to visit him at his new address.

No More Doubts

Agnes, his first wife who was living in southeast England, felt considerably shaken on learning that John was still alive. Agnes assumed that he had drowned because the morning after he left, his hat and wallet had been found beside a riverbank. She had annulled their marriage and had remarried a devoted carpenter who remodeled their home into a dream cottage. The peace and joy in this new relationship had rid her of any animosity toward John.

All three of the people in this intriguing story managed to find closure. For Agnes, the mystery of John's disappearance, which had often disturbed her peace of mind, was solved. For John, there was the relief of confession, forgiveness and the assurance of Ellen's love. For Ellen, the nightmare of separation and doubt had ended. A new day had dawned, and John and Ellen renewed their vows in a second wedding ceremony.

Lt. Colonel Bramwell Pratt's story appeared in his book, God's Private Eye. *He headed The Salvation Army Investigation Department for 23 years.*

One Father, Two Sons, Three Continents

Reported by Ken Ramstead

R obert's decision to stay in India rather than return to England after World War II would forever change the trajectory of his life and the lives of those closest to him. He asked his wife to join him along with their two sons, John and Peter, but she didn't want to uproot the family.

Two years later, when he returned home, his wife refused to see him. Hoping to speak to his sons, he went to their school. But the headmaster, on instructions from the boys' mother, refused to let him see them. Distraught, but seeing no alternative, he returned to India.

Although Peter and John's mother eventually divorced Robert and remarried, "we never referred to our step-father as 'Dad,'" said Peter. "There was never any doubt that we had a father, and that he was in India."

Over the years, both boys moved away from the family home, married and raised families of their own. Peter left England and settled in Canada. While Peter and John occasionally speculated on their father's whereabouts, friends convinced them that it would be useless to try and search the records in India.

Australia

Much to their surprise, 59 years after they last saw their dad, John received a letter from The Salvation Army in London. Their

92-year-old father was still alive and well near Sydney, Australia. He had moved there from India, remarried, and wanted "to make peace with his two sons after all these years."

"We thought he was dead," said Peter.

Despite their initial reservations, Peter and John decided to call their father. "I didn't know quite what I was going to say," recalled Peter, "so when I dialed and he picked up the phone, I just asked if he was Robert and when he said, 'Yes,' I replied, 'Well, this is your son, Peter.' It was an emotional chat and I could tell he was near tears."

One telephone call led to another, and before long Peter stepped off the train in Springwood, New South Wales, Australia, for a long-awaited reunion with his father.

A Second Family

Robert had told his Australian family, including two sons and a daughter, about Peter and John, his two older sons in England. But he gave them no details about his previous marriage, or growing up in England with his parents and siblings. Given the circumstances of his departure—the animosity and devastation—he wasn't sure how any contact from him might be received. He was worried that the subsequent turmoil might have a negative effect on both his English and Australian families. Since he'd already lost one family, he didn't want to risk losing another. "He felt so very guilty that he never contacted us over the years," said Peter.

> "He felt so very guilty that he never contacted us over the years."

After his second wife died, Robert remarried and continued to hide his secret from his third wife for another 25 years. Racked by remorse, he finally confessed to her. Then they began a search through The Salvation Army in Australia, which culminated in a reunion with John and Peter.

"As it turned out, Dad was somewhat surprised and quite proud to find out my brother and I hadn't turned out too badly after all," chuckled Peter.

The reunion has been positive for the extended family. They keep in touch with one another on a regular basis, and John and Peter plan to visit Australia together. Their new half-brothers and half-sister have also expressed an interest in visiting England and Canada. The wounds of a lifetime have finally healed.

"Our only regret is that it took so long," concluded Peter.

Ken Ramstead's story appeared in the Salvation Army publication, Faith & Friends, *in Canada.*

The Photograph

Reported by Betty Anderson

L ars and Inger belonged to the first wave of European immigrants who came to the United States seeking a better standard of living. They married on board a ship while travelling from Sweden to the United States. After their relationship foundered and Lars left Inger, she returned home to the old country and gave birth to their son, Max. In 1921, when Max was seven years old, she sent him to America to live with his father, hoping to offer him the future that she and Lars had longed for together. She resumed her own life and eventually gave birth to another son.

Economic Downturn

Eight years later in 1929, the stock market crashed, followed by the Great Depression, and Lars, like many people, could not provide for his son. He was placed in foster care and in several orphanages. Max felt abandoned by both of his parents. Eventually, a caring, supportive family adopted him and he managed to work his way through college. He had no further communication with his family in Sweden, and they couldn't locate him in America.

More than 60 years went by. Max's brother died in Sweden, and he was named as a beneficiary in the will. His brother's attorney contacted The Salvation Army to initiate a search for Max, who was by then 80 years old. The Army discovered that his last name had been changed when he first arrived at Ellis Island as a small boy.

> ## This small gift enabled him to put the past behind him.

With the help of the local police department, The Salvation Army managed to find him, but the pain and anger of abandonment had hardened his heart. He had no desire to reconnect with his Swedish family. It seemed that too much time had gone by for him. The Salvation Army officer in charge of the case, on reading his life story, had found no mention whatsoever of a family in Sweden. He had completely written them out of his life.

Kindness

Fortunately, a simple yet poignant act of kindness made all the difference for Max. The thoughtful attorney took the time to send him a photograph of his brother and his mother. As soon as he saw it, his attitude started to soften. This small gift enabled him to put the past behind him, and the old wounds slowly began to heal.

Major Betty Anderson serves as director of The Salvation Army Missing Persons Bureau in West Nyack, N.Y.

A Fond Farewell

Reported by Anthony Robinson

I'll never forget the day my dad and I were reunited. I was extremely nervous because I hadn't seen him in more than 50 years. Many questions about my childhood remained unanswered. Because my dad was very ill, I wondered how he would respond to me. Would our encounter heal the wounds of the past?

Jack and Audrey, my parents, had married in Bermuda, but their marriage failed before I was born in England. At that time, Jack was serving in the British merchant navy and sailing extensively throughout the world.

Losing My Hero

Meeting him for the first time when I was 10 years old, I clearly remember being awestruck by this man who resembled a movie star to me. Although Jack wanted to reconcile with my mom, she was unwilling to move to Bermuda.

Jack's departure upset me. The promise of a fuller, happier life had been dashed and I was left without a father. We corresponded until my mother remarried and the new family arrangement discouraged any contact with my father. I often wondered how he was doing and how he might feel about the possibility of a reunion. Would my attempt to reach out be rejected? Would old wounds be reopened? How would other family members react?

A few years ago my wife, Marion, and I discussed the possibility of a vacation in Bermuda, intending to make a few discreet inquiries as to Jack's whereabouts. Unfortunately, this trip never materialized.

Imagine my feelings when I received a letter from The Salvation Army in London informing me that Jack was seriously ill in Vancouver, Canada, and wanted to see me. For 50 years I had waited for this invitation. Without hesitation, Marion and I made the trip to meet him.

Saying Goodbye

When we arrived, Jack was quickly slipping away. There was so much I wanted to say, but because of his illness, verbal communication was limited. Nevertheless, I felt great emotional relief as wounds of the past were healed. I met Jack just in time to bring him peace of mind and to assure him of my love.

> For 50 years I had waited for this invitation.

Our departure was difficult. I knew I would never see him again, but the reunion changed my life. It brought me a feeling of inner peace and completion, which I'm sure he shared.

After Dad died, I celebrated his life with many relatives in Bermuda. Through our brief, eleventh–hour encounter, I became connected to an extensive new family in Canada, the United States and Bermuda. I used to be an only child, but now I am part of a large and diverse family.

I am grateful to my sister in Vancouver and to The Salvation Army for making my dream a reality.

Anthony Robinson's story appeared in the Salvation Army publication, Faith & Friends, *in Canada.*

Putting The Pieces Together

Reported by Monica Housman

"Y ou have a brother out there somewhere—go and find him," Mary said as she lay dying. These were the last words she spoke to her daughter Joy.

Joy was left behind to grieve with a lot of questions and no answers. "My mother just left me hanging," she said. "It was great news, but I was so hurt—she gave me nothing to go on."

That wasn't the first time Joy had heard whispers about a mysterious older brother. When her father died, her mother let it slip that she had put a child up for adoption when she was 19 years old. "She said a few words about it and then refused to mention it again," Joy said.

That same year, 1,100 miles away in Indiana, Joy's older brother Richard was grieving the loss of his adoptive father. It was the first of many coincidences the siblings would uncover when they met for the first time at Joy's home in Orlando, FL.

Richard's Childhood

Richard grew up in the small town of Wakarusa, IN. His adoptive parents told him the story of going to Grand Rapids, MI, on Valentines Day, in the middle of a snowstorm, to pick him up when he was only a few weeks old. "The battery fell out of their car after they got me and they were stranded," Richard said.

Richard remembered a happy childhood with loving parents. He knew that his birth mother had been young and that her parents had been unkind to her when she became pregnant. He believed that she had given him up in his best interest. "I was never mad at her or anything," he said. He never felt an urge to track down his biological mother, mainly because of the close relationship he had with his adoptive mother and father.

He grew up as an only child, had two children and later married his current wife, Esther, who had five children of her own. Richard managed a trucking company and Esther worked for The Salvation Army in Goshen, IN.

Health Issues

After Richard's adoptive father died, he began having health problems. The bevy of doctors he consulted all asked the same question: "What is your family history?" Richard and Esther decided it was time to begin the search for Richard's birth family in earnest.

Richard's adoptive mother had never encouraged him to search for his origins before he became ill. "I believe she always had that fear deep in her heart that his real mother would come along and take him away," said Esther.

But once Richard's health was at stake, she gave him her unconditional support. She died one month before Richard found his biological family.

Richard knew that his adoption had been handled through the Elkhart County Welfare Department, even though he had been born in Grand Rapids, MI. County adoption records were sealed, however, which meant that another avenue had to be pursued.

Coincidences

Richard had obtained his birth certificate from the state of Michigan through a fluke. "They aren't supposed to send you your birth certificate if you're adopted," he said. "But somebody must have goofed, because they sent mine to me."

When Esther opened the mail that day, the name on the birth certificate excited her so much that she immediately called Richard at work. His mother's name was listed as Mary Louise—and

Richard had named his first-born daughter Rosina Louise. "It was such a neat coincidence," said Esther.

Another coincidence would lead to Richard's reunion with his sister. His wife Esther had worked for The Salvation Army for 25 years, and one day she said, "Wouldn't it be weird if you were born in a Salvation Army Booth Maternity Home?"

"It was just an offhand remark, and we didn't think anymore about it," Richard recalled.

Esther forgot it until she was stymied at every turn by a number of agencies refusing to release adoption records. On the slight chance that Richard's mother had given birth in an Army hospital, Esther decided to write to Booth Records in Chicago. The shocking news came back that Richard had indeed been born at a Booth Home in Grand Rapids.

> With health problems of his own, it was time to begin a search for his family.

Still, only certain "non-identifying" information could be released. Richard and Esther learned that his birth mother had received some help from relatives in Elkhart during her pregnancy, which explained why the Elkhart County Welfare Department had handled the adoption. They also learned that his birth mother had named him Robert Ray before his adoption.

They saw written proof that Richard's biological mother had not wanted to give him up. But there was no information on his birth father, and although some of his curiosity had been assuaged, he was not much closer to finding his mother.

An Obituary

With the help of a missing persons caseworker, the couple finally obtained a newspaper obituary for Richard's birth mother, Mary Louise. They quickly scanned the list of survivors and discovered that Richard had a sister named Joy Horton.

Even with Joy's name and address, it was no easy task to find her. She and her husband Kevin moved throughout Florida several times before The Salvation Army finally located her in Orlando. Joy had five children and 14 grandchildren, and all of them were eager to meet Richard. The first rendezvous took place in Orlando, followed by a visit to Goshen from Joy.

Additional sleuthing may be in store, because Richard's mother had lived with an aunt and uncle just before he was born.

"It would be interesting to see what other relatives I have right outside my back door," he said.

"He Looks Like Grandpa"

The first comment Joy's children made when they met Richard was, "He looks like Grandpa." Richard had been searching for his birth mother, but after meeting with Joy and her family, it began to seem like he had uncovered his birth father's identity as well. Joy and her relatives were amazed at the similarities between Richard and her father, Robert—the way they walked and the shape and size of their hands.

Same Mother And Father?

The discovery that Richard's birth mother had named him Robert Ray before he was adopted became even more significant. Family members who could have confirmed whether Richard was Joy's full brother were all dead, but the siblings are convinced that they share the same mother and father. "There are just too many things that show that he is Robert's son," said Joy.

The most logical scenario, according to Esther, is that Mary and Robert had met and conceived a child outside of marriage and that Robert, who was in the Air Force, had not forgotten him.

Joy had noticed that her mother would become depressed at the beginning of February—when her son would have celebrated his birthday. "It always seemed like a hard time for her, but I didn't know why," she remembers. And Joy understood why her mother insisted on calling Joy's daughter, Rachel, by the nickname Ray—the middle name she had given her son.

Unveiling so many major secrets has taken a notable toll on Joy. Her happiness at finding the brother she had always wanted is laced with anger at her parents (now both dead) for keeping his existence a secret for so long.

Joy had felt very close to her parents, especially since she was—or so she thought—their only child. Now Richard and Joy are making up for lost time, together healing old wounds and learning how to be brother and sister.

"All of this has been made possible by God's grace," says Esther. "We thank God for our counselor on the missing persons staff and all her love, care, prayers, and hard work."

Richard with his sister, Joy

Editor's Note: Despite difficult psychological and legal issues, overwhelming numbers of adoptees and birth parents are seeking contact, and adoption professionals are becoming increasingly responsive to their needs. Release of contact information between adoptees and birth parents legally depends on the consent of the parties involved. But even if The Salvation Army is unable to supply information to those seeking a reunion, it can still provide an emotionally safe and neutral ground for the parties to meet. Regrets are extremely rare and reunions are here to stay.

Monica Housman's story appeared in the War Cry. *Photo by Jeff Arbogast.*

A New Dimension

Reported by Ruth Miller

'T'he discovery of my daughter and my grandson has added a new dimension to my life in terms of completeness," said 70-year-old John, a financial consultant living in Hartsdale, NY.

For 45 years, the missing piece had been Gina, his daughter conceived during a wartime romance, when American soldiers were not allowed to marry citizens of foreign countries. John, stationed in London during the Korean War, had wanted to marry his girlfriend, but his superiors wouldn't give him permission. "Before I knew it, they had put me on a plane back to the United States," he said.

Seven months after he returned home, he learned of Gina's birth. Only 22 years old, he felt overwhelmed by the situation. "I communicated with Gina's mother for five years and then we drifted apart," he said. Eventually, their contact ceased altogether and he retreated into his work. John married, but his marriage lasted only two years.

Trip To London

"I made several attempts to locate Gina and her mother," he said. "After a visit to London and an extensive search, I concluded that they were no longer living there." Actually, Gina's mother was still in London, but her daughter had moved away. She had been working around the world as an anthropologist in Australia, Ghana, and Liberia.

A few years later, a breakthrough occurred when Gina, now a real estate broker, initiated her own search for her father. After exhausting all of her European resources, she contacted The Salvation Army in the United States.

A Faded Photo

Gina recalled that, "All I had to go on was this wallet-sized photo of Dad taken 45 years ago and the stories my mother had told me." The faded, well-worn picture showed a headshot of John in his military uniform. Normally, the Army would not have accepted her case because she had such sparse information, but after learning the vast extent of her search, the Missing Person's Bureau moved ahead on her behalf.

> "All I had to go on was a photo of Dad in his military uniform."

"I received a letter from The Salvation Army inquiring whether I was the person being searched for, and that if I thought I was, to call back for further details," John said.

He was told of a young woman in London who might be his long lost daughter.

"Upon calling, I reached Gina's mother and later spoke with Gina," John said. Frequent communication followed.

The Big Apple

Finally, father and daughter met for the first time in New York City. "We spent a week together, getting to know one another," John said. "I didn't want to intrude on her life. But when we met, we just knew that we belonged together."

Gina, by now married and divorced, returned to New York a few months later for an extended stay of three weeks.

"I'm at peace now," John said. "I'm not searching for anything anymore. I just hope that I can make her life a little better."

John and Gina participated in the production of a national video for the Missing Persons Bureau in the hope that more people would come forward and tell their stories.

A Mid-Life Crisis

Reported by Bramwell Pratt

T o this day, I can recall somewhat nervously knocking on Kathleen's front door and showing her my Salvation Army credentials. Her familiarity with The Salvation Army put us both at ease, and I wasted no time revealing the purpose of my visit. Many missing persons naturally confide in a neutral party once they trust that their confidentiality will be respected, and she was no exception.

Swept Off Her Feet

Kathleen was a married woman in her forties who had been working as a nursing orderly in a hospital in England. Her daily routine bored her and she felt taken for granted by her husband. Like many people who reach her age without resolving significant issues, she struggled with a classic mid-life crisis. When a male patient in his sixties began to flirt with her, she felt overwhelmed by a surge of obsessive love that blocked her ability to think rationally. She convinced herself that time was running out and that she had to change the course of her life.

George was a charming, vivacious extrovert who had no trouble convincing Kathleen to move away and live with him once he regained his health. Within a few short weeks, however, the romance and excitement of the relationship faded, and the harsh reality of

Kathleen's impulsivity hit home. She thought of her husband often and sadly conceded that she had made a big mistake in leaving him. She grieved for the safe haven of her comfortable middle-class life. In no way did her new lifestyle compare with the one that she had carelessly tossed aside.

A Second Chance

Meanwhile, Kathleen's husband John sought the help of The Salvation Army to find her. His willingness to initiate a search convinced her that he still loved her and wanted to give their marriage a second chance. She decided to tell George that she was going home to John.

> Her new lifestyle could not compare with the one that she had carelessly tossed aside.

George, who had been married 40 years, turned out to be equally repentant. Returning home from work, he admitted that he had treated his wife poorly and expressed a desire to reconcile with her if only she would forgive him. "There's no fool like an old fool," he lamented.

Three weeks later, a Salvation Army representative working in the vicinity decided to visit the homes of Kathleen and George, where he found them reunited with their respective spouses. He offered a simple prayer of thanksgiving that both couples had been given a chance to start over.

Never Giving Up

Reported by Dorothy Post

"**I** hope you don't come back. My mother and I could really use the insurance money!" These caustic words from Fred's wife dealt a crushing blow the day he left home to serve overseas in the U.S. Army. They came as a surprise, too, because until then he had believed that he and his wife were happy together.

Fred and Alice first met when she moved to Washington, D.C., to work as a secretary during World War II. They fell in love, married, and had a baby daughter, Beverly. They were a real family—or so Fred thought.

World War II

During the four years he fought in the Pacific—from the Philippines to Japan—he wrote to Alice faithfully. None of his letters were ever answered. With classic understatement, Fred said of her lack of concern, "It wasn't very morale building."

Still, when he left Fort Dix, NJ, with an honorable discharge and his old job waiting for him at the Navy Yard in Washington, D.C., hope was uppermost in his mind. He headed straight for New York City, where Alice and Beverly lived with his mother-in-law. On the way there, Fred allowed himself to imagine the happy life he and his family might have in store.

Reality couldn't have been more different. No loving embrace greeted him, and no tears of joy were shed for his safe return. Alice had no intention of moving back to Washington and setting up a home with him. Life had been easy for her while he was away, she said, because her mother wouldn't let her do anything except take care of Beverly. "I can't see keeping house for a man," she told Fred bluntly.

Losing Touch

Fred's marriage, which had begun with love and commitment, lay in ruins. Nonetheless, he hoped that at least he and Beverly would remain close. It distressed him, though, when his daughter called him Fred, instead of Dad, during the day they spent together at the Bronx Zoo. When he reminded her that he was her father, she insisted, "No, my daddy was killed in the war."

Fred had no way of knowing that 56 years would pass from that day until the next time he saw her. At first, he sent checks to Alice to support his daughter, but every one of them was returned unopened. "She was determined to lose contact with me," he said. To Fred's sorrow, her efforts succeeded only too well.

Fred's later search for Beverly was relentless. "I tried for years to find my daughter," he said. "I contacted agencies that claimed they could find people anywhere, and I found out that they just bleed you for money. They keep telling you, 'Oh, we're getting close. Just send us $150 more.' "

What Fred couldn't have known was that Beverly never stopped looking for him, either. As a much loved only child in a household with her mother, aunt, and grandmother, she was showered with gifts and attention. But nothing diminished her longing for her father.

"I wanted to find my dad all my life," she said. "In the beginning, they told me he died in the war. But I was a stubborn little girl. I said, 'If he died, I need to see his body.' It was something I felt in my heart."

Resistance

When she was old enough to read, she found a letter from Fred expressing a desire to see her. Her family conceded that he was alive, but the picture they painted of him was dark. "I got a lot of negative feedback about him," Beverly said. "But he was always in my heart, and I wanted to hear his side of the story. I wanted to re-unite my mother and dad all the time when I was young. And I always wanted brothers and sisters. I had this dream of bringing them together, but it never came to pass."

Over the years, Beverly asked permission to find her father. "But my mom never encouraged me or allowed it." Even so, when she traveled to other cities for school trips, she would pour through telephone books looking for his name. She found other people with the same last name, but she couldn't summon the courage to call them.

> Nothing diminished her longing for her father.

Alice's resistance to a reunion continued even after Beverly became an independent adult. "I'm sure he's gotten married again and doesn't have time for you," she warned. Because Beverly loved her mother and didn't want to hurt her, she obeyed her wishes.

Remarriage

In fact, Fred had remarried. The happy life he had dreamed of was realized with his new wife, Linda, and the eight other children that made up their family. "We've been married for 43 years," he boasted. "And we're trying to hit 50."

After years of leads that failed to materialize, Fred's son took the search on-line. Through the Internet, he learned that Alice had died in 1998 and that the rest of her family was also deceased. Knowing that Beverly had been left alone in the world intensified Fred's resolve to find her.

During a stepdaughter's visit with Fred and Linda one Christmas, the conversation turned to the ongoing search for Beverly. To Fred's surprise, she asked, "Have you tried The Salvation Army?" Like many people, he had no idea that the Army was in the business of finding missing persons. But since every other search had led only to a dead end, Fred thought he had nothing to lose. He contacted The Salvation Army in the Chicago area.

The Army called Fred two days after his 80th birthday to say that Beverly had been found. Eagerly, he asked for her address and telephone number. His spirits sank when he discovered that the policy of the Missing Persons Bureau was to contact the missing person first.

The Stroke

Then Fred sent an important message to Beverly through The Salvation Army. He had suffered a heart attack and a stroke that had left him paralyzed, but he assured her that he didn't need anyone to take care of him. What he sought was not a caregiver, but a relationship with the daughter he had always loved.

When Beverly received a letter from the Army saying someone was looking for her, she felt suspicious. Except for her husband's prompting, she might never have returned the call from the Missing Persons Bureau. When she learned that her father was the person searching for her, emotion overwhelmed her. "I thought I was going to pass out!" she recalled. "Because I always wanted this."

Even so, she didn't call her father that day, rationalizing that she would have more time to talk on the weekend. Now, she confesses, "I got cold feet. I was scared. I wanted to talk to him, but I didn't know how he would feel about me." The next day, she received another call from the bureau and was told, "He's sitting by the phone waiting for your call right now."

The Conversation

The immediacy of those words spurred Beverly to action. She told her husband, "I have to call my father right this minute." When Fred answered the phone, a wonderful memory was awakened. She remembered his voice!

"It was a beautiful feeling," she said. "We must have talked for about two hours. We exchanged addresses and he told me he would love to see me. And I was so anxious to see him."

"It was something," Fred agreed, "after 56 years."

A month later, Beverly visited Fred and Linda on Father's Day. "He rushed out to the car," Beverly said, "and we hugged for what seemed like 10 minutes! We were so happy to be together."

The rest of the family also welcomed her with open arms. "I call my stepmother Mom now, since my mom has passed away," she said. "And when my baby sister Janet met me for the first time, she cooked dinner and gave me a cake that said, 'Welcome home, Beverly.'"

Wholeness

"When my mom passed away, it was like the end of my family. I adopted myself into my husband's family because they're very loving and wonderful. But now I have so much more family! We have half–siblings and step–siblings but we don't even talk about that, because we're all brothers and sisters. They're beautiful people, and I feel very comfortable with them."

Since their first reunion, Beverly has visited Fred and Linda several times. "I had Thanksgiving with all of them last year. It was wonderful." With such a large, extended family, she has not yet met everyone, but she looks forward to getting to know each one.

Fred remarked that their reconciliation has "filled a hole that was there." For Beverly, it has also healed many wounds. "It's closure for me," she said. "I've watched Montel Williams and Maury Povich—all those people who've had reunions on television. I've sat there and cried and wished it were me. I'm sorry this didn't happen a few years before, but while my mom was alive, it couldn't have happened. I feel great."

A BBC Reunion

Reported by the Family Tracing Service Review in London

"Y ou reach a stage in your life when you need to know answers. You're prepared for rejection and things not working out, but you have to know," Carol said. Her attempt to find her father, Ken, was filmed by the British Broadcasting Company for a documentary, and was revisited in a British television series called *Missing Live*.

Carol didn't find out about her biological father until she was in her twenties. He had moved away when she was a child. It was only when she was getting married and needed her birth certificate that her mother told her about him.

The Wedding

"I had a happy childhood and grew up in a very loving family," Carol recalled. "When Mom told me about my real dad I was surprised, but I had no desire to find him. We were all happy the way we were."

Seeking out her biological father was awkward for Carol while her adoptive father was still alive. The years went by, she married and had her own family. Then she discovered that Ken had served as the best man at her aunt and uncle's wedding. "The family hadn't mentioned him out of respect for my mother and her new life, but it seemed he was a decent man. They all spoke highly of him," she said.

"Two of my children were getting married last year and it was my aunt and uncle's golden wedding anniversary—so the time seemed right to start looking for Ken."

Television Documentary

Carol's search through The Salvation Army's Family Tracing Service was featured in a BBC One documentary called "Reunited" just prior to Christmas.

She didn't mind being filmed while searching for her father. "I wanted to find my real dad, and agreeing to take part in a documentary was something I felt I might as well add into the pot of my emotions. It was nothing compared to what I had already gone through to prepare for finding him."

The search for Ken took the Family Tracing Service three months. Then Carol and Ken exchanged letters.

"I started to write a letter," recalled Carol, "and it took me ages. What on earth do you say after more than 45 years?"

Pictures

"He wrote right back, and my husband told me I had to call him. I hate phone calls. I tried to put it off, but finally he sat down with me while I dialed the number. That first call lasted one and a half hours. It was amazing—as though we really knew each other.

> "What on earth do you say after more than 45 years?"

"Next came the face-to-face meeting and I burst into tears. It was so emotional. Ken was super. He'd brought old pictures of my childhood and that was a great icebreaker.

"Now I feel complete and really happy. We're all very close. Ken, my aunt and uncle and I all talk every week. I've met his extended family and it's lovely for my children, even though they are grown-up, to have grandparents.

"Taking part in the documentary was a good experience. I suppose the questions they asked made me think about my situation and better prepared me for finding Ken and eventually meeting him."

The Missing Piece

Ken was equally delighted to have found Carol again. "I never stopped thinking about her," he said. "Carol was always a part of my life, and she was never a secret from my family. I would think about her on every birthday and during special occasions. I wanted to be part of her life, but I didn't know how to be. I worried I'd upset her.

"I was nervous at our first meeting. I worried that I wouldn't be the person she was expecting, but we're both very open and everything just fell into place. Everything seemed quite natural. Having contact with Carol has made my life complete, more rounded. The missing piece is now back in place and the number of my grandchildren has grown from 12 to 18!"

Carol with her father, Ken

Letting God Do The Impossible

Reported by The Salvation Army's Chicago Office

V) ernice and her brother Robert sat together on the sofa in a Salvation Army center, anxiously awaiting the arrival of their two younger brothers. They had seen photographs, so they knew what to expect, but they were still feeling antsy about the big moment when their siblings would walk through the front door. Being on camera for a missing persons video did little to abate their uneasiness.

"I'm overwhelmed!" Vernice said, wringing her hands together. "I can't believe this is happening." Blessed with a strong maternal streak, she had missed being a big sister to her younger brothers for the past 27 years.

The Oath

When their mother grew ill, she moved from Arizona to San Antonio, TX, to be near Vernice and Robert. It was then that the family discovered that she had terminal cancer. After her surgery, the doctors predicted that she didn't have long to live. Vernice promised her mother before she died that she would find "the boys." This pledge gave her mother hope and helped to prolong her life. But it wasn't until five months after her death that her two younger sons were located.

"It's kind of a bitter sweet occasion," noted Robert, who is pensive and soft-spoken. "I wish our mother were here to greet them."

"We'll have to get to know each other as adults," Vernice pointed out. "People change a lot when they grow up. I don't even know their favorite colors or what food they like."

Vernice and Robert sat almost on the edge of their seats with their backs to the door. When they heard the door opening, both stood up and turned around to embrace their brothers, who were dressed in baby blue clothes and wearing cool sunglasses. Vernice was ecstatic, and Robert looked teary eyed.

Enjoying The Moment

"What happened?" Vernice teased. "Either you shrunk or I grew!" she said to the shorter of the two men. Turning to her other brother, she said, "You look just like your dad."

> "All you have is your family. We need that bond."

While the four siblings grasped hands and reverently bowed their heads, Vernice offered an emotional prayer of thanksgiving for their long-awaited reunion. Then they took a trip to the cemetery to visit their mother's grave.

"All you have is your family," said Vernice, beaming. "We need that bond."

"We never gave up hope," Robert said, while the three brothers reminisced with their sister over old photo albums. "People can do what's possible, and then they have to turn the situation over to God. We have to let God do the impossible by answering our prayers," he said.

Thirty Years Of Tears

Reported by Colin Fairclough

Twenty-year-old Jeannette made front-page news after eloping with David, the 19-year-old son of her parents' gardener, who was working as a building apprentice. Jeanette was the daughter of a military officer, the British Army's head of physical training and an aide-de-camp to the Queen of England. Her parents were staunchly opposed to her marriage.

The Cut–Off

While the couple was living in London, a daughter, Suzanne was born. But as soon as the honeymoon ended, their relationship began to sour. Jeannette left home, and Suzanne remained with her father, eventually becoming a ward of the court in the care of her paternal grandparents. David's parents blocked all attempts by Jeanette to see Suzanne. From an early age, they told their granddaughter that Jeanette had died of pneumonia while Suzanne was still a baby.

At the age of 16, while she was rummaging through her grandmother's papers, Suzanne found her parents' divorce documents. When she raised the issue, she was told that her mother was a very wicked woman, and that she was better off without her.

"Never a day went by that I didn't think about her," admitted Suzanne, "but I always felt angry towards her because that was the way I had been programmed to think."

Thirty years after her mother left home, Suzanne asked The Salvation Army to trace her. Holding pictures of Jeannette from old newspapers, she told an Army caseworker, "I have cried so many tears – 30 years worth. After so much misery, happiness has to be the reward. I would give up everything to be with her. I never married, so that my name remained the same in case my mother tried to find me."

> For a few brief days, she had the experience of loving and being loved.

The twists and turns in Jeannette's life made the search difficult, but a few months later the Army found her living in London. Although she was delighted to hear of her daughter's inquiry, she was also extremely shaken. When Jeanette called Suzanne the next day, Jeanette was very drunk. Their relationship seemed off to a rocky beginning.

A Tearful Reunion

Nevertheless, they arranged to meet on a Saturday afternoon at the train station, where Suzanne would be arriving from her home. She was told to "look out for the woman with the red purse." The two met with warm, tearful embraces. They spent the whole next day telling stories, setting the record straight, expressing remorse, and sharing much love and understanding. Two lonely women had found the greatest joy their hearts had ever desired.

Tragedy Strikes

The next day, Suzanne returned home, planning to re-visit her mother the following weekend. She called her mother a couple of times early in the week, but on Wednesday Jeanette did not answer the phone. Fearful that she might be sick, Suzanne jumped into her car and drove to London through a blinding rainstorm. When her mother failed to answer the doorbell, Suzanne left the apartment and called the police. Within minutes of arriving, they moved quickly through the house to find Jeanette lying dead on the kitchen floor. The doctors later said she had suffered a massive stroke. She was only 52 years old.

In Suzanne's life, a great work of emotional healing had taken place. For the first time, albeit for a few brief days, she had the experience of loving and being loved. She began using her mother's maiden name and continued to keep in touch with The Salvation Army. She has often said, "No one can take her away again. And I know that my mother was happy for the first time in 30 years."

Jane Doe

Reported by Ed Forster

H er green plastic hospital wristband seemed to shout it—"Jane Doe." She had been admitted to the hospital at midnight with a head injury. The hospital staff referred to her as Jane Doe because she had no identification or personal recollections.

The nurses had put her to bed with the hope that all would be well in the morning. When the sun rose, it brought the police with a bundle of questions. Their inquiries fell helplessly into the chasm of a true identity crisis.

Captain Kirk

The auburn-haired, hazel-eyed Jane could supply only two fragments from her past. She remembered the name Captain Kirk and the city of Bath, ME.

Bath was 150 miles from the bridge that spans the Merrimack River in Manchester, NH, where she had slipped on the icy pavement and struck her head the night before. Captain Kirk, of course, was light years away on a remote Star Trek planet.

The Bath Police Department couldn't shed any light on Jane's identity. They had no report of a missing person fitting her description, although they had found Captain Kirk. He was a Salvation Army officer in Bath.

Curtains surrounded Jane's bed, but because of crowded conditions, she was situated in the hallway.

"I'm Captain Forster," I said, as I extended my hand. The woman's grip and her expression were both filled with questions.

"I'm from The Salvation Army," I said, hoping for a flicker of recognition. After a moment's pause, which seemed much longer, I asked, "Do you know about the Army?"

She searched the darkened closets of her mind, and then said, "No. I don't think so." My assumption that she was a Salvationist had been wrong.

I considered asking her more questions, but I could see that her energy had already been drained by police inquiries. A tear trickled down her cheek, and she didn't brush it away. Perhaps she was hoping that I wouldn't notice.

"Someone must be looking for me," she said. "There must be a family I belong to." Her wedding ring suggested that this was true.

A phone call to Captain Kirk brought me no closer to a solution because neither he nor his wife knew the woman I described.

A Thank–You Card

"A gift," she said, as I came back to her bedside. It was time for me to wear a confused expression.

"My family got a thank-you card from someone in Bath for a Christmas gift that we gave them," she explained, excited over this new clue. "I remember the postmark on the envelope. Will that help?"

"I'm sure it will," I said. In truth, my heart didn't hold the confidence of my words.

Valerie, a young woman from Manchester, was working with The Salvation Army in Bath. Hoping she might prove to be our missing link, I called her and explained our dilemma. Her only guess was that she might have worked with Jane Doe at a laundry in Manchester. She arranged for another employee from the laundry to come to the hospital and help us identify Jane Doe. My excitement and joy nearly turned to despair when that person told me, "I've never seen this woman before in my life."

Phone Calls

Valerie was anxious to solve the mystery, but she didn't have any other ideas.

"Do you have an address book in your purse?" I asked.

"Yes," she said. "Why?"

"Please open it and thumb through it. Give me the names of anyone who might remotely resemble Jane's description."

It was a long process. Each time someone on Valerie's list answered the phone, I'd breathe a sigh of relief and explain my reason for calling. All of them were sympathetic, but none could offer any further clues toward solving the puzzle. The nurse at the hospital had said that state investigators would have to be notified if no answers were found by the end of the day.

One More Try

On my last try, a teenaged girl answered the phone.

"Is your mom at home?"

"No, she isn't."

"Do you know where she is?"

"No, we don't," the trembling voice answered.

"Did your mom come home last night?"

The girl was near tears. "No, she didn't. We thought that she went to visit a friend, but none of her friends know where she is." She began to sob.

"Your mom's all right," I assured her. "Tell your dad to meet me at the medical center in 20 minutes. He will know me by my Salvation Army uniform."

When we walked into the hospital room, Jane looked directly at me. She didn't seem to know her husband at all.

> "Someone must be looking for me. There must be a family I belong to."

Moment Of Truth

He reached for her, and she pulled back and screamed. Patiently, he took her hand and patted it slowly. She became calmer. The silence continued for several minutes as the attending nurse and I watched and waited for something to happen.

Suddenly the woman burst into tears and reached out to embrace her husband. The light had finally returned to brighten her darkened memory. The Jane Doe wristband could be discarded. She was back in the arms of someone she loved, and who loved her.

The nurse and I left the room quietly. We spent a few moments in the hallway praising God and rejoicing over one who had been lost, but now was found.

Major Ed Forster served as a Salvation Army corps officer in Manchester, NH.

Trading Places

Reported by the War Cry in Australia

F or 20 years, Tracey had answered the telephone at work, listening attentively to strangers tell their stories of hope and heartache.

As a caseworker for The Salvation Army's Family Tracing Service in Australia, this mother of two has reunited hundreds of loved ones separated by time, misunderstanding and family breakdown.

Tracey empathizes with the sorrow of those searching, counsels people through the tentative first contact and rejoices with reunited families. She also consoles those who discover it is too late for that longed for reunion—either a loved one has passed away or, perhaps worse, doesn't want contact.

To say that Tracey's job is emotional would be an understatement. Day after day of wading through the broken lives of other people would drain even the most emotionally detached individual. But the empathy Tracey affords strangers on the phone is much more than a professional courtesy.

A Happy Childhood

After piecing together the emotional jigsaws of countless lives, Tracey knew it was time to answer questions about her past. It was time to search for her biological father.

Her upbringing was extremely happy, and she always felt surrounded by love. "My interpretation of a dad is in my heart," she said, clutching her hands to her chest. Although her biological father, Robert, left the family when she was still a toddler, Tracey's mother remarried and she considers her stepfather, Bill, to be her dad.

Growing up, Tracey never felt a burning desire to trace Robert. The subject rarely arose, although she does recall one family argument when she learned the truth. "When I was about seven years old, we were at the park and an argument took place between Mom, Dad and my grandmother. That's when I found out that Dad wasn't my real father." But even this revelation had little impact on her young life, said Tracey.

"As a young child I didn't understand it. It was never hush-hush about Robert, but it was hardly ever talked about, either. I grew up with a very happy childhood with a lot of love and never had any interest in this man who wasn't there."

The Right Time

Love and loyalty have been strong influences in Tracey's life. Not until her mother's death did she seriously begin to consider searching for her father. Her stepfather had died when she was 14 years old.

"I've always felt loyal to my mom, but with the work I'm doing we only ever hear one side of the story of broken relationships," she said. As time passed, Tracey realized that the advice she had been giving to others applied to her, too.

"I'd been speaking to children from broken marriages looking for a parent—and one lady told me a story that sounded very much like my own. Her father had left home when she was a baby, and she had grown up with her stepfather. Her mother had died 12 months earlier. The moment I heard her story I said to her, 'It's obviously very important for you to hear your father's side of the story.' As soon as I said those words, that was it.

"I count that as a real God moment for me. All this hidden anger, resentment, all the questions—I felt it just release from my body. I thought, 'You're telling this lady to do what you should be doing yourself.' I felt at peace with the whole situation and thought, 'Yes, I'm going to do it.'"

The process of tracking down Tracey's father was relatively easy. A distant cousin provided a starting point, and within a few weeks she had found an address for him.

But she had had enough experience with family reunions to know that finding a missing person is often the easy part. Actually making contact is a lot harder. Tracey used her work address as the return contact on the envelope. After a few weeks elapsed, she concluded that her father didn't want to see her. Then one day a letter from him arrived.

> "I had a very happy childhood and never had any interest in this man who wasn't there."

"I guess the first emotion I felt was relief," she said. "It's very hard to deal with the disappointment when the person we are looking for has died, because then there's no closure."

Three Questions

In her letter to Robert, Tracey asked three questions: *Do you know how old I am? Do you know my birthday? Do you have a photo of me?*

If he could answer yes to just one of those questions, she thought, she would feel an emotional connection to him.

"When I started reading his response, I felt almost paralyzed. In the end I had to get a co-worker to read it for me. It was all a bit of a blur, but I remember the answers to my questions were no, no and no. I felt very disheartened."

The co-worker encouraged Tracey to call her father, but she knew she needed time to think. "I didn't want to rely on a knee-jerk reaction, so I prayed to God and thanked Him that Robert was alive. Eventually I called him and I was very upfront. I said that I was really disappointed that he had responded 'no' to my three questions. If he had said 'yes,' I would have felt like he cared about me."

Robert explained to Tracey that, although he didn't have any photographs of her, he could remember exactly what she was wearing the day he left. Tracey says that meant a lot to her. "That softened me. That image had stayed in his heart and mind forever—maybe he did care about me."

After that first phone call, Tracey and Robert talked on a regular basis. A few months later she, her husband, and two children met with him. She said she didn't know what to expect at their initial meeting.

"When we were walking up to his place, I was worried that I might have a heart attack. Then the door opened, we fell into each other's arms and I just couldn't let go. Eventually we went inside and stayed for about three hours."

Now What?

Tracey is well aware that people can get caught up in the emotion of finding a loved one, only to feel confused when reality hits home. "I'm 43 years old and he's a stranger, so—after the initial outpouring of emotion—I'm finding it hard to forge a deep connection. When people ask me if meeting him was what I expected, I have to say that I didn't know what to expect."

"Since meeting Robert, my husband has told me that he always sensed something was missing in my life. He said that after I met Robert, the need he felt in me was no longer there. He feels that I'm complete now."

Tracey at her office in Australia

Three Aunts

Reported by Douglas Peacock

R on was born in a Salvation Army Booth Maternity Home when adoption records were still kept tightly sealed. At the age of 58, he contacted the maternity home, which sent him some generic information about his birth and his mother. Finding that his birth records could not legally be opened, he decided to let the matter drop. Ten years later, however, he changed his mind and contacted the Booth Hospital Records department of The Salvation Army.

Booth Records

Booth Hospital records are a throwback to an era when women secretly gave birth at Salvation Army maternity homes to avoid the stigma of pregnancy outside of marriage. While these centers didn't actually handle adoption services, Army staff helped to place the children through various other social service agencies.

As society's mores gradually changed, acceptance of single mothers and the advent of birth control began to reduce the need for these services. By the mid–1970's they had either been closed or remodeled for other purposes. Booth Records, however, can still house relevant information that might reunite children with their parents.

Since Ron's birth mother would have been 90 years old, there was only a slim chance that she would still be alive. Rather than try to find her, he asked The Salvation Army to connect him with anyone in her family. Through Ron's aunt, Alice, the Army learned that his mother, Jane, had died more than 10 years earlier. At first, Alice seemed wary of any contact with her nephew, but she agreed to send him a photo of his mother as well as other information about his family. Ron responded with a letter and a photo of himself, which appeared to ease her anxiety.

> Nothing had brought him more joy than being reunited with his birth family.

Eventually, Alice shared the news of Ron's inquiry with other relatives, along with his photo and letter. Alice and her two sisters then made plans for Ron to visit them. The three women, all in their late 80's, were the only family members who had known about Ron's birth. "You're part of our family now," his aunts assured him as they introduced him to his other relatives.

Although Ron grieved because he would never meet his mother, nothing had brought his life more joy than being reunited with his birth family.

Major Douglas Peacock serves as the director of the Missing Persons Bureau in Long Beach, CA.

Old Soldiers

Reported by The Salvation Army's Chicago Office

A Chicago caseworker glanced up from her desk to see an elderly man standing patiently in her doorway. In his hands he held a crumpled piece of paper and his eyes were filled with hope. The tattered sheet held the names and service numbers of his Air Force crew—members of Lt. General James Doolittle's Silver Bombers during World War II, and three men he desperately wanted to find. He had been to the Red Cross and the Veterans Administration, but they weren't able to help him. If anyone could find his missing crew members, he was sure The Salvation Army could. He had a special affinity for the Army because of the humanitarian role it had played during the war.

John didn't have dates of birth or any other clues to move his case forward. The missing persons' caseworker, distracted by the piles of paper overflowing on her desk, doubted that she could do much to help him. She could either tell John that the Army didn't pursue this kind of search, or she could make a couple of calls and see what turned up. One look at his expectant face, and her decision was made.

She learned that between 1955 and 1997, all three of his friends had died. There was no easy way to break the news, and John didn't respond well. He started shaking, thanked her abruptly, and rushed out of the office. The caseworker grabbed two cups of coffee, caught up with him, and offered him a shoulder to cry on.

Pocket Watch

Then John began to reminisce. He pulled out his treasured pocket watch, which had stopped at exactly 11:16 a.m. on April 25, 1945, during the last bombing raid on Germany. As the senior officer in command, he was at least 10 years older than the other men. They had teased him and affectionately referred to him as "Pops." He felt proud of the fact that they had all returned home safely. A large reunion had been held in Las Vegas, but John, recovering from a heart attack, had been unable to go. He later learned that none of his crew had attended, either, and he had been looking for them ever since. How could he have outlived all of the men who had flown with him?

> ## His pocket watch had stopped at exactly 11:16 a.m.

He talked about his wife of more than 50 years, whom he still referred to as his "bride," and their two children—a daughter, who worked as a pediatric nurse, and a son, a physical therapist for the elderly.

John had come to The Salvation Army for help in finding his three missing friends. He had felt the need to talk about old times with his Air Force crew, but he made some new friends who were willing to listen. When he finally left the office, he felt at peace. He continued on his way to the nursing home where he made some routine stops to see family and friends.

The caseworker's day hadn't gone as smoothly as planned. Her desk was still piled high with case files and her phone was ringing. But she hoped that God had used her to comfort John in his sorrow. She got her answer the next day when he returned to her office with a box of candy and various newspaper articles on his historical bombing mission. Once again, he voiced his appreciation for The Salvation Army, "It seems like it's always there when I need it most," he said.

When Brian Met Sally

Reported by The Salvation Army's Chicago Office

Brian and Sally were inseparable friends who grew up together in the same neighborhood. In their late teens, they had planned to marry, but when Sally became pregnant their lives were torn apart. Both sets of parents seemed determined to drive a permanent wedge between them. Sally's parents sent her away to have the baby and give it up for adoption, while Brian's parents pushed him to join the Coast Guard.

A couple of years later Sally married, desperately wanting another baby. Although she was never happy with her husband, she was a faithful wife and the mother of five children. Twelve years later, her husband left her. All of Sally's children knew about Brian and the child who had been placed for adoption. Once her divorce was finalized, they encouraged her to look for him and their daughter. Sally took their advice and contacted The Salvation Army for help.

Brian was shocked when the Missing Persons Bureau contacted him, but he was delighted that Sally was looking for him, and he could hardly wait to see her. He would have searched for her when they were younger, but he didn't know how and as time went by, he feared disrupting her life. His heart's desire had been to marry her and raise a family together. Brian had eventually married another woman, although he had been a widower for four years when the Army found him.

> ## Sally was the woman he should have married.

He immediately called Sally and arranged to meet with her. When they saw each other face-to-face it was as though no time had passed. They became reacquainted and met each other's children. Although Brian had loved his wife very much, he always believed that Sally, his first love, was the woman he should have married. Clearly, they were meant to be together. As this missing persons case came to an end, a fairy-tale wedding was well underway.

A 40 Year Embrace

Reported by Fonda Marie Lloyd

V ivian fondly remembered a 13-year-old boy who helped her sneak rides on her father's workhorses when she was 10. They stole cigarettes, smoked, and drank coffee together in order to feel grown up.

Her memories of the boy, her brother, kept Vivian searching for him. Her search ended when she embraced Lawrence for the first time in 40 years.

Greener Pastures

The two were separated shortly after their widowed father, who had seven children, married a woman with four children. Neither Vivian nor Lawrence got along well with their stepmother. When Lawrence was a young teenager, he moved away from the family's Missouri farm to live with one of his brothers. At age 20, he joined the Navy.

Vivian, meanwhile, left home at age 16 to live with an older sister in New York. She never saw her brother after that, and eventually they lost track of each other. Vivian then began to search for him. Though she had married and moved to California, she continued the search, combing phone books and asking relatives if they had heard from him or knew of his address. For years she heard nothing.

"I looked for him for many years and there'd been a lot of prayers and a lot of worry," she said.

While living in Washington, D.C., Vivian saw the name and address of The Salvation Army Missing Persons Bureau in a Dear Abby newspaper column. The contact information was an answer to her prayers.

Within an hour she was on the phone. She sent the bureau an application fee and a copy of the last letter she had received from her brother 33 years earlier. Then she waited.

Five months later she received a call from Lawrence's wife, Margie. She and Lawrence, who lived in New Hampton, NY, had received a letter from the Missing Persons Bureau, asking if he wanted to be reunited with his sister.

"She started to cry and I started to cry," Margie said. "We were babbling for 20 minutes to half an hour. We couldn't get any talking done."

Catching Up

Lawrence and Vivian eventually got to hug each other in the driveway of her home. "I was on cloud nine that day," Vivian said. "Forty years is a long time without your brother." The 13-year-old boy she remembered had become a father of four children as well as a grandfather.

> The 13-year old boy she remembered had become a father and a grandfather.

Vivian had changed as well, Lawrence said. His little sister, with her long auburn hair, was now a widow with two grown sons. She wore her graying hair short.

It had been a long time since they were 10 and 13 years old when Lawrence had smacked the horse she was riding and screamed "Hi Ho Silver." She had fallen off, but they agreed to tell their father that she had fallen out of a tree.

I teased her after that and said, "Hi Ho Silver, Kerplop!" laughed Lawrence.

Vivian cooked a meal that had been their childhood favorite, and they caught up on the four decades they had been apart.

"I hope we have another 40 years to be together," he said.

Fonda Marie Lloyd's story appeared in The Times Herald Record, *Middletown, NY.*

Fireworks On The Fourth Of July

Reported by Tom Lamarra

When children of divorce are born to different sets of parents living in separate cities, they may not even know that they have siblings. Edith, Bill, Dottie, and Susan remained in the dark about each other until they were grown and married, with families of their own.

After Edith's parents divorced, she went to live with her biological father in New Jersey. Her mother, Maybel, remarried and had two more children, Bill and Dottie, who were born in Camden, NJ. After the second marriage failed, Bill and Dottie went to live with foster families. Maybel moved to Chicago, married a third time, and had another daughter, Susan.

Dottie had wanted to search for her siblings, but the search upset her foster parents, so she called it off. After they died, she redoubled her efforts to establish contact with her family. She wrote a letter to Edith by way of The Salvation Army, which obtained her Social Security number and then forwarded the letter to Edith's former employer.

An Elephant's Memory

Although the employer didn't recognize Edith's maiden name, "Jones," he remembered her and forwarded the letter to her. "I had worked with him, and I was the only Edith he knew," she explained. She didn't hesitate to follow up on the lead.

Meanwhile, Maybel, who was near death in Chicago, called Dottie and revealed that she had another sister, Susan. "I met my sister Dottie at Mom's funeral," Susan said. "But we had talked on the phone previously."

Bill, who lived in South Carolina, had already been in touch with Dottie. Now that all the siblings were in touch, the table could be set for a family reunion on the Fourth of July. But the Independence Day reunion turned out to encompass a much larger group than just the four of them. Edith now had four children and two grandchildren. Dottie had two children and one grandchild, and Bill and Susan each had two children. Not only had they found each other, they also inherited a number of nieces and nephews.

> "What's amazing is that we're alike in so many ways."

"You want to touch, you want to feel, you want to hug—you want to touch them to see if they're for real," said Susan when she came face to face with Dottie, Bill, and Edith. "It's freaky to go from being an only child to being the baby in a family of four. It's nice to know there are more people in the world that you have something in common with, but you're worried about acceptance," she said. "What's amazing is that we're alike in so many ways."

Portraits, Photos, Pillow Fights

The new family had a portrait taken and even enjoyed a pillow fight. "We're reliving our childhoods," said Edith.

Susan finally saw a picture of her mother when she was a child. "I was so excited," she said. "I wasn't mad or upset that Mom didn't tell me about Dottie, Edith and Bill. It was like a whole separate life for her in New Jersey."

Dottie and her siblings were eager to find out more about their mother's life. They knew about a second brother, Franklin, who had died when he was just five years old. But their birth certificates listed different numbers of children in the family. Although one birth certificate states that Maybel had seven children, only five are accounted for.

"It's all speculation," said Dottie, "but there is a period of 16 years that is completely blank. There could be two more children out there." All four siblings seemed determined to solve the mystery.

Tom LaMarra's story appeared in the Bridgeton, NJ, Evening News. *Photo by Gary Cooper.*

Dottie, Edith, Bill and Susan

Banished

Reported by Colin Fairclough

T oday we find it incredulous that a perfectly sane person could spend most of a lifetime confined to a mental hospital. It's almost unheard of for someone to be forcibly detained for psychiatric treatment, with the exception of a court-ordered alternative either to prison or a criminal trial. In fact, we often witness just the opposite—people who desperately need help fall through the cracks to commit violent crimes that might have been avoided through professional intervention.

As recently as a generation ago, however, patients' rights were not so readily protected. Not only in the movies was it possible for an unwanted person be banished to an insane asylum. A case in point concerned a young woman named Arexie, who was robbed of a normal life until a caring social worker finally took positive steps to set her free.

A Courtship In Turkey

After World War I, Arexie fell in love with a British soldier who was stationed in Constantinople, Turkey. She and Albert married and returned to England, where Arexie gave birth to a daughter.

Apparently Albert lost interest in Arexie, who spoke very little English. Then he tried to get her certified as insane, but private physicians refused, declaring her sound in body and mind. Finally, he persuaded a military doctor to give her a false diagnosis of schizophrenia and commit her to a mental hospital. Their five-year-old daughter, Joan, was placed in a convent. She later rejoined her father after he had begun living with another woman. Joan assumed that her mother had died.

> ## "I just couldn't believe that she'd been locked away for 63 years."

Many years later a social worker befriended Arexie, by then in her nineties and living in a mental hospital in England. As they chatted in French, Arexie revealed that she had a daughter who would be almost 70 years old. Without even a name or date of birth, the social worker asked The Salvation Army whether there was any hope of tracing her daughter. A short six months later, Joan was found living on the coast of England.

Joan excitedly tells of the hugs and kisses the first time she saw her frail mother, sitting alone in the ward of the hospital.

"I just couldn't believe that she'd been locked away for 63 years. A whole lifetime! There are no signs of insanity. She's fit and well, and she doesn't even need medication."

Universal Language

Arexie's English was mixed with Armenian, Turkish, French, and Arabic, but the language barriers melted away as she conversed easily with her daughter and granddaughters. "It's good," she said, "everybody smiles at me, and is so kind."

Joan arranged for Arexie to move into a nearby residential home, and soon she was able to enjoy walking along the ocean while eating ice cream and popcorn!

Joan also obtained her mother's wedding ring, sealed in an envelope with her hospital records. She declared, "Mom's life story reads like the plot of a best-seller. Truth certainly is stranger than fiction! I won't let her go again."

Tearing Down The Wall

Reported by Dorothy Joy

H awaiian sunshine filtering through the flowering vines on the patio couldn't brighten the darkness of Luella's depression. She basked in the exuberant growth of the garden, where hibiscus and oleander bloomed and palm trees swayed, dancing a ballet to the wind's tune.

Then she turned to the shadowed spaces of the living room. White walls, white rugs, exotic peacock colorings of furnishings and drapes, a dramatic modern mural of flaming orange, scarlet, and black, were all muted by the subdued light coming through the louvered screens.

An Unexpected Visitor

As she flipped through the pages of a magazine, she heard the distant sound of the doorbell. She glanced at her watch and registered the fact that the houseboy wouldn't have left. He would see who was there.

Then she heard the pad of his slippers as he crossed the hallway. He stood in the open doorway of the room and waited for her to speak.

"Yes?" She looked at him with a question on her face.

"A lady. She says her name is Mrs. Graham."

Luella's first reaction was to say that she didn't know any Mrs. Graham. She didn't want to see anyone. The depression, loneliness, sadness—it would be hard to put a name to her feelings—had a palpable weight that she couldn't seem to shake. She felt incapable of speaking to anyone. But an almost unacknowledged curiosity made her change her mind.

"Okay. I'll see her."

Luella moved slowly toward the door, her expression changing as she caught sight of her visitor. A red badge made a splash of color on the white uniform, and a quick smile took the place of an introduction.

"But I don't know"– and then the ungracious words were halted as the woman smiled again.

"But of course you don't know me. I'm Vinnie Graham, and I'm from The Salvation Army. And I've been looking for you for hours!"

"For me?"

The Right Luella

"I'm certain of it. You're the fourth Luella Markham I've contacted, and you're the last one in the directory, so you must be her.

"The one?" Luella was mystified.

Vinnie looked into the hard, yet lovely face. "I'm looking for someone who used to be Luella Bennett."

The change of expression on Luella's face, the sharp intake of breath, the quick hand movements, answered the query more surely than words.

"You are Luella Bennett?" Vinnie gave the woman no time to reply. "Good. Then I can give you a message from your mother."

"I—I have no mother."

Vinnie made a mental note of the disclaimer and continued speaking. "She's in the hospital in New York. She has a terminal illness, and she's asking for you."

"Whoever this woman is, she can ask as much as she likes. She's not my mother." The statement sounded final.

"But –"

Luella amended her statement. "By birth, maybe, by pain, by flesh and blood. But not by love and caring, not by sympathy and compassion. Rather than have the trouble of my upbringing—washing my clothes, combing my hair, comforting me—she gave me away. It might have meant problems for her, but she would have none of me."

"Oh, no!" Vinnie's comment was a long-drawn sigh.

"Oh, yes. An aunt gave me all I needed, except a personal mother-love that was mine alone. I was rejected."

"You have so much now."

Wall Of Pride

"Yes, a husband who loves me, a beautiful home, even children of my own, but I still carry the shame of that denial with me. I won't see the woman who calls herself my mother. I've rejected her, as she did me. You can say that to whoever sent you to me."

There was an upsurge of sympathy in Vinnie's heart as she looked at the woman's proud face. Could she pierce this hardened façade? She prayed again as she spoke.

"What a pity that you've gone to such pains to build a wall of partition."

"It's a wall that will never be broken," Luella said. She moved impatiently, restless under Vinnie's direct gaze.

"You've built a barrier—indestructible—you say—between yourself and your mother? You've added to it through the years, and you've nearly destroyed yourself and all you love, all that is good in your life. Now with one quick decision, all that could be erased—but the decision must be yours."

> "Whoever this woman is, she is not my mother."

Vinnie rose to go, reaching as she did to take the other woman's hand, and as she turned to the door, she looked behind her. "There's a seat booked for you on a flight to New York at 8:00 p.m.," she said confidently. Then she was gone.

There was less confidence in Vinnie's voice as she told the story to her husband.

"She was hard—and who could blame her? I can understand her feeling of not being wanted by the one person on whom she felt she had a personal claim—the one to whom she really belonged. She's built up an impregnable wall."

Flight To New York

An hour later, as they sat down to supper, the telephone rang. When Vinnie heard the caller's voice, she held the receiver so that her husband could listen to the conversation.

"Louella?" There was a new quality in the voice that was almost unrecognizable.

"Vinnie, I just wanted to tell you that I'll be on the 8:00 flight." There was a pause. "Thank you for helping me to break down the wall, or at least to begin the crumbling process."

Dorothy Joy's story appeared in the War Cry.

A Railroad Rambler Returns

Reported by Robert E. Thompson

C harles, a Newark, NJ, toolmaker and the father of five children, had had it. He left home.

"I was an alcoholic and I just got up and left," he said. He was not defensive, not trying to make an excuse. He was just stating a fact.

From his old home in Newark, Charles hit the Bowery flophouses in New York and worked on the railroads along the Eastern seaboard. "First, the Lackawanna, then the Pennsylvania—in New Jersey and New York—I was even on the Boston & Maine."

Army Jobs

After five years as a railroad employee he ended up at The Salvation Army Adult Rehabilitation Center in Buffalo.

"I didn't stay there long," he said. The wanderlust still gripped him.

Around the time he first went to work for The Salvation Army, he tried to get in touch with his family. He wrote a letter to his old Newark address, but the family had moved, and the letter was returned stamped "unknown." He assumed that his family had no interest in seeing him again and made no further effort to reach them.

Later Charles worked for The Salvation Army in Ohio, Pennsylvania, and Indiana as a plumber, cabinetmaker, radio repairman and red shield donations truck driver. He liked being a truck driver because it was a "responsible job."

The Stroke

After he suffered a stroke, his good friend, a Salvation Army captain, took him to the hospital. Paralyzed on his left side, he went to live in a county nursing home. "I thought of trying to go home, but I didn't think anyone would want me. It was a long haul and I couldn't work," he said.

While he recovered in the nursing home, his family, remembering his past connection with the Army, contacted a state social service agency in Newark and then the Army's Missing Persons Bureau in New York. Before long he was located in Ohio.

Another Addition

Charles' five children and his wife Margaret got on the phone to greet him. He was thrilled to hear from them, but he didn't want to go home—he'd be a burden. They talked. "They're persistent kids," he noted.

> "I thought of trying to go home, but I didn't think anyone would want me."

Shortly after Christmas all of his children arrived in Youngstown. "My prayers have been answered. This is the best Christmas present ever," Charles said.

About midnight on New Year's Eve, he was at his wife's new home. There was a stranger waiting for him. It was 18–year–old Mary Ann, a daughter he had never seen before. His wife had been expecting her at the same time Charles left. Also in the area were 21 grandchildren who would soon meet their new grandfather.

Robert E. Thompson's story appeared in the Newark News *and the* War Cry.

Together After 81 Years

Reported by Colin Fairclough

H enry was a British soldier who had no idea how to be a father to two boys and a girl after his wife died.

All of the children had been born on foreign soil—Harry, the oldest, on a military base in the British Isles; and William and Elsie May, in Cairo. Upon returning home to England, Henry left military service and resumed civilian life as the manager of a boarding house in England.

He sent Elsie to live with an uncle when she was about two years old. That was the last contact Elsie had with her father and her brothers.

When she was 83 years old, her son Brian asked The Salvation Army to trace her family. Her husband had died a year earlier, and she still felt strongly that she was the child who had to be "given away." Would it be possible to trace her brothers or, more likely, their descendants?

The necessary details surfaced very quickly. Elsie's mother had died of blood poisoning, leaving her husband, Henry, to raise three small children alone.

The first family member located was Ada, the widow of Elsie's brother Harry, who had died seven years earlier. Ada provided a telephone number for her brother William. William had a photograph of the entire family taken before their mother died, which he was eager to show to Elsie May.

The Same Nose

Brian took his mother to meet William in England the following weekend, just 15 days after the inquiry began. William placed both hands on his sister's shoulders, looked her in the eye, and said, "Elsie May, you must be one of us, because you've got a big nose like I have!" No other aside could have been a better icebreaker. Soon the two of them were chatting away as though no time had elapsed.

> "You must be one of us, because you've got a big nose like I have!"

The reunion story was later included, along with a photograph, in the Guinness Book of Records. It was also featured in many national and local newspapers. The Salvation Army gave Elsie and William a kitchen towel that included a picture of them to mark the occasion.

Elsie Mae, Major Colin Fairclough, and William

A Roller Coaster Ride

Reported by Casey Alston

T)he caller ID on my living room telephone read "California," and I knew immediately who was on the other end of the line. This long-awaited phone call marked the end of more than 47 years of separation and 15 years of intermittent searching.

"This is Ric. I'm your father," the voice on the other end said.

"Well, I've been waiting a long time to hear that!" I replied in my usual flippant way. Our conversation lasted about 30 minutes. Just like old friends, we talked about anything that popped up. Was it just nervous chatter or a genuine connection?

A Birth Defect

I hadn't considered trying to find my father until my daughter Amber was born with a partial cleft lip. After her birth, I realized that a piece of *me* was missing; therefore, a piece of my children must be missing, too. We needed medical history from someone I didn't even know.

The breakup of my parents had left my mother filled with bitterness toward my father. The only time his name ever came up was in a negative context. I had only a handful of clues that might lead me to him——my birth certificate, a couple of pictures, and not much else.

I remembered that he used to pilot helicopters and that he had written to me from California. He had contacted my maternal grandparents, but they had misled him and had shattered his hopes of finding me.

I contacted the Salvation Army's Missing Persons Bureau to ask for help. Around that same time I was also leaving on vacation for Santa Monica, CA. I felt strongly drawn to California on that trip, for reasons I would understand later. The next year, while preparing for another trip there, I submitted the necessary paperwork to the Missing Persons Bureau and launch an official search for Ric.

My letter, the first of three, was bitter and offensive. The Army urged me to soften it and try to make it more welcoming. The second letter requested medical information that I needed to help treat Amber's condition. I also uncovered a lead through the Federal Aviation Administration that helped move the case forward. Yet more than a month went by with no results to report.

Then I called the Army to say I had moved and to give the bureau our new address and phone number. "We're pretty sure we have the right person," I was told, but there was still no word from my father.

A Visceral Message

I drafted a third letter, this time a heartfelt one sharing personal details about my kids, my job and my innermost feelings. It noted the irony that both my husband and son now worked in the aeronautics industry. The letter included pictures of myself, my husband, my children and stepchildren, and even the dog.

A couple of months later Ric called the bureau and a caseworker read my letter over the phone to him. He and Laurie, his wife of eight years, had just returned from a 10,000-mile camping trip across the United States. He freely discussed his other children, his reason for lack of contact, Laurie's openness to a reunion, and his willingness to reconcile.

In weeks to come, Ric and I would exchange numerous emails and talk on the phone as often as three times a day. My first conversation with Laurie, which was intended to be a quick hello, lasted 20 minutes and ended with potential plans for a family reunion.

A Cross–Country Trip

During his trip in a recreational vehicle around the country, Ric had visited the children of his middle son, Shawn, from whom he had been previously estranged. Shawn also reunited with our father a few years ago, and he's given me lots of insight into our family. Ironically, Ric's travels had taken him practically into my own backyard, with a chance to cross paths in five different states.

The widening of my family circle has enriched my life immensely. In addition to my siblings, I now have three brothers, a sister, a brother-in-law, a sister-in-law, a niece and her family, and Laurie's daughter Jamie.

Emails are flying, traits are being matched, and we have moved beyond the past. You know, I thought I had it bad to have to tell my mother and stepfather about finding Ric. But he has risked a lot more. He risked being totally rejected by his wife and four children, once they found out I existed and the circumstances involved.

> Finally Casey drafted a letter that shared her innermost feelings.

My family is making plans to fly to California for a preChristmas visit with Ric. It's been one wild roller coaster ride, a ride I wouldn't have missed for the world. I feel like the man I'd never seen before has always been a part of me. And always will.

Casey Alston submitted this story to The Salvation Army's Long Beach, CA, office.

A Palpable Connection

Reported by Colin Fairclough

W hen siblings are separated from each other, for whatever reason, there is cause for real sadness. And when those siblings are twins, the sense of loss is even more palpable. The story of Barbara and Philip, who had been apart for 70 years, is cited in the Guinness Book of Records.

Philip wrote to The Salvation Army in search of Barbara. He told the Army that his mother had placed an advertisement in The London Times seeking an adoptive family for the twins when they were babies.

"The ad was answered by my adoptive family. My twin sister was sent to live with relatives. When I was 14 years old, I learned that I had been adopted, but nothing was said about a sister. Ten years ago I found a number of letters sent between my adoptive mother and my birth mother that mentioned a sister. I wonder if it is possible to trace her."

A Mother's Plea

Philip and Barbara's mother had sent the following letter to Philip's adoptive parents:

"I received your letter today answering my notice in The Times, and will explain the circumstances that led to it. A year ago my husband died in an accident, and six days later, I gave birth to twins, Philip and Barbara. A few months later, I entered the hospital with pneumonia. My illness, combined with the shock of my husband's death and the birth of the twins, has left me very weak.

"As soon as warm weather arrives and I regain my stamina, I'll need to resume teaching in order to provide for myself and my other two children, who are nine and 11 years old. With two babies, I can neither grow stronger nor return to teaching. I've been urged to place them in an orphanage, but I've resisted as long as possible, because babies need tender care and the comforts of home.

"However, it's essential that I do something. So, as a last resort, I tried running the ad you answered. I'm prepared to surrender them absolutely, and whoever takes them can rest assured that there'll be no interference once the babies have left my care . . ."

Further letters in immaculate handwriting were sent routinely to the family, including details about the babies and other relevant information. When Philip was a year old, both sides agreed that he alone would be adopted.

Reticence

By now a senior citizen, Philip decided to look for his twin sister, and a local agency referred him to The Salvation Army. It was possible that Barbara also had been adopted and that her name had been changed. A search began for information about the other children in their birth family. The Army found a birth certificate for their brother, Charles, who was 81 years old. When the Army contacted him he was extremely guarded, and he asked Philip several questions before agreeing to communicate with him.

> "I am quite prepared to surrender them absolutely. Rest assured that there will be no interference."

Charles wrote: "More than 70 years have elapsed since Philip left our family. As he was taken while my older sister and I were living with relatives, following the death of our father, neither I nor my sister ever saw him." Despite his reservations, however, Charles did confirm that he was in close touch with Barbara, now married and with three children, and also with an older sister, a nun living in Rome. Their mother had been dead for 35 years.

After a round of reassuring correspondence, Charles, Barbara, and Philip met exactly 70 years to the day after Philip was adopted. Barbara's daughter attended the reunion, as did Philip's wife.

Intimacy

Although Charles was somewhat reserved, the warmth between the twins was impossible to miss. "I felt a strong emotional bond as soon as I touched Philip's hand," Barbara said. "It was a marvelous and wonderful thing," echoed Philip.

The story of Barbara and Philip appeared in many newspapers, and they were interviewed together on radio and television.

Barbara later informed The Salvation Army that Philip had died. "But," she added, "before he died we wrote to each other every week without fail. There was such a lot to catch up on."

The "Other" Sister

Reported by Susan Randall

F ifty-seven-year-old Marie was looking for a sister she'd never met, when a third sister named Sarah (born Gladys Alfreida) found her. "We sound alike," Marie said. "We laugh alike. We have the same interests. And she was also known as 'the mouth.'"

Marie knew that her older sister, Judith Kay, had been adopted, and she had hoped one day to trace her. But she doubted that she would ever find her other sister, Gladys Alfreida, because she knew only her name and her birthplace – at the Salvation Army's Booth Hospital in Chicago.

One day Marie got a call from an employee at The Salvation Army's Booth Records office in Des Plaines, IL. "She knew my full name, my mother's maiden name, both of her married names, my grandfather's name, where my mother and grandparents were born, and that I had two sisters, Judith Kay and Gladys Alfreida. I told her I'd been searching for Judy for years, but The Salvation Army had said they couldn't give me any information on Gladys."

"I Don't Cry Easily"

"Well, Gladys just found you," the records officer told her. "Would you like her to call you?"

"Oh, yes!" Marie agreed. "By now, I'm crying," she said. "I don't cry easily, but the tears were flowing at that point."

"I didn't even know I had a younger sister," said Sarah, who was 60 years old. Sarah had contacted The Salvation Army after her son developed a familial disease and she needed the family's medical history. Then the Army found a copy of her mother's death certificate signed by Marie. When Sarah called Marie, they talked for more than two hours. "She asked me what color my hair was," Marie recalled. "I said, 'blonde out of a bottle.' She said hers was, too."

"I picture our mother on a pedestal," Sarah told her.

"She was," said Marie. "A bar stool!"

"So Mom kept you?"

"Actually she tried to get rid of me, too, but I came back," Marie said. "She told me I was kidnapped by the babysitter when I was a baby, and they didn't get me back until I was three years old."

Waiting

The two sisters met for the first time in Casa Grande, AR. "We talked three times on the phone before she came out here," said Marie, who was up at 5:00 a.m. for a 1:00 p.m. rendezvous.

Marie and her husband, Wilton, two of their four children, Rob and Tanya, and two of their seven grandchildren, five-year-old Britanny and two-year-old Brandi, arrived early and waited an hour past the rendezvous time at a rest stop on Interstate 10 north of Casa Grande. They were on the lookout for a 38-foot recreational vehicle (RV) from Michigan that never showed up.

"I was raised as an only child," Marie said as she waited. "To know I have two sisters out there and not have a clue as to where they are, it's kind of haunting. I don't know how she feels about me, but I feel like I've already bonded with her."

A call on Tanya's cell phone finally ended the wait. Sarah and her family had mistakenly driven to another RV park about two blocks from Marie and Wilton's home north of Casa Grande. When Sarah stepped out of the RV and Marie emerged from the car, the two women looked so much alike that no one could doubt they were sisters.

"You're so little," Sarah told Marie as she threw her arms around her.

"I can't believe I've finally got a sister," Marie said. "I'm still the baby, but I'm no longer an only child." "You know," she quipped, "the mayor is afraid you're going to settle here."

Dead Ringers

"Can you imagine the two of us in the same town?" Sarah asked, and the two sisters broke into peals of laughter. "Well, we do look alike."

"Same sense of humor," Marie added with a nod.

Marie gave Sarah a photo album of her children, her grand-children and her own childhood – "so she could see how I grew up." Sarah handed Marie a picture her granddaughter had drawn of the two sisters meeting for the first time. It showed Sarah in shorts and sandals, and Marie in a short skirt and high heels.

"I told her you were little and wore a size five shoe," Sarah said. "She kept telling me to call you and ask you what you looked like. This is very overwhelming," she said, wiping away tears.

"There was no way I ever dreamed that Sarah would be found," Marie said in amazement.

"How old was Mom when she died?" asked Sara.

"Seventy," Marie answered.

Together the sisters peered at a photo of their mother holding a baby that Marie believes is Sarah. "That's what I looked like, too," Marie said, "bald and round faced."

"I think I need more Kleenex," Marie said.

After Sarah talked to Marie for the first time, she told her adoptive mother that she had found her sister. "I was a little apprehensive about how she would feel," Sarah said. "But she said, 'I think it's great. Tell her I like her already.' My adopted sisters are thrilled, too."

> "To know I have two sisters and no clue as to where they are is haunting."

Getting Acquainted

Sarah and her husband, Mike, live in Stevensville, MI, only two hours away from Chicago, where Marie and her husband

Wilton lived until they moved to Arizona. Sarah grew up on a farm, the oldest of five children. She and Mike own a small amusement park on Lake Michigan and a tool-and-dye shop. Marie, by contrast, had grown up on the streets of Chicago. She is a court appointed special advocate for children.

"It's like a dream," Marie said. "It really is. You've seen this happen to other people on television, but you never think it will happen to you." As Marie's granddaughters shyly approached Sarah, Marie reassured them. "You can call her Aunt Sarah now, " she said.

"My granddaughter, who is 11 years old, had no girl cousins," Sarah explained. "She's so excited about you."

Mike showed the girls a photograph of young children standing in the snow. "These are all your cousins. Five of them." Overcome by shyness, the little girls hid their faces behind their mother's legs.

Wrinkles

"See," Sarah said, turning back to Marie, "I got the wrinkles, too. We must have inherited them from our mother. And the chicken neck!" The sisters broke into more peals of laughter.

"My daughter noticed that we have the same body language," Marie said. "Our hands move and we rub our necks while we're talking."

"I think it's wonderful to find a sister I didn't know I had," Sarah said. "I'll be meeting a lot of new relatives, too."

"I knew about you," Marie said, "but all I knew was your first name and where you were born."

"What was my name?" Sarah mused. "Gladys Alfreida! Thank goodness my mother changed it!"

Sarah and Marie continue to search for their older sister, Judith.

Susan Randall's story appeared in the Tri Valley Dispatch, *Casa Grande, AZ.*

Calm After The Storm

Reported by Douglas Peacock

T he Salvation Army received minimal information from Isaac to trace his immediate family—his parents' names, his brother's name, and his place of birth. He couldn't even recall the birth dates of any of his relatives. "I didn't participate much in family gatherings," he explained in his letter to the Missing Persons Bureau in Long Beach, CA.

The bureau worked feverishly to locate his brother, his sister Erica, or anyone else who might be a link to his lost family.

Isaac, a native of Louisiana, had left home to join the Air Force. He'd been out of touch with his family for about 30 years while serving time in prison.

Hurricane Katrina

Meanwhile, the bayou state was slowly recovering from perhaps the biggest disaster in its history—Hurricane Katrina—and thousands of families had been separated after a mass evacuation that scattered refugees all over the United States.

Erica's daughter, Sarah, called the bureau, tearfully explaining that no one had heard from Isaac in a long time. Her entire family had been torn apart after the hurricane, and she had no idea where any of her other relatives were living. Sarah agreed to pass on Isaac's contact information to Erica.

Louisiana was recovering from perhaps the biggest disaster in its history, Hurricane Katrina.

Through his sister Erica, Isaac was reunited with his father and another sister and received pictures of them. He continued to write to The Salvation Army, expressing his appreciation for their work and updating the Missing Persons Bureau on the latest news of his family.

"It sure is a blessing, a priceless gift that I have received from God," he said. "I've also been informed by my sisters that I have 42 nieces and nephews! It was a delightful shock. Thank you again."

No Longer Lonely

Reported by Kathy Lovin

More than 40 years ago, Tim's parents, alcoholic and destitute, made a difficult choice. They gave up three of their six children to be adopted by other families. Tim and two of his sisters left their birth family and went their separate ways with adoptive parents.

In Tim's new family, there were five girls. They'd had a brother who died at birth, and Tim saw his adoption as an attempt to replace the lost son. Try as he might, he just couldn't fill the boy's shoes.

Hard Knocks

Physical, mental and sexual abuse filled Tim's early years. Once he became a teenager, he rebelled and suffered the consequences—prison. Upon his release, he moved to Yakima, WA, to start a new life.

More than 25 years later, he reflected back on a life that had perpetually challenged him. He suffered from drug and alcohol abuse, stints of homelessness, multiple marriages, and bouts of depression and loneliness. "I've graduated from the school of hard knocks with a black and blue diploma," he said.

Yet, as is often true when people endure suffering, Tim had also been on the receiving end of God's abundant grace. Throughout his struggle, he felt the call of God on his life and a passion to share the Gospel with others. He prayed that someday he would find out more about his birth family and reconnect with them. Tim also prayed for someone to talk to, someone to keep him from dying of loneliness.

Friendship

God answered his prayers by bringing 97-year-old Rose into his life while he was washing dishes at The Salvation Army. Rose was lonely, too, aside from needing a full-time caregiver. Suddenly, Tim found a new job caring for her, as well as the support and companionship he'd always longed for.

> "I would have paid a million dollars to find my family."

Rose, who was active in The Salvation Army, urged Tim to contact the Missing Persons Bureau to help him find his family. Once he filed the necessary paperwork to open a search, the Army spent nearly a year tracking down his siblings. When Tim received the good news, he felt thrilled but a little overwhelmed.

Now he is in telephone contact with two of his sisters. He has also recently met his older brother, Curtis, in person after more than 40 years. Together, they plan to travel to the East Coast to visit their sisters.

It has been a healing process for Tim. "I would have paid a million dollars to find my family. This is priceless," he said.

Tim and Curtis share a lighthearted moment.

Kathy Lovin's story appeared in the New Frontier, *a newspaper published by The Salvation Army in Long Beach, CA.*

My Long Lost Valentine

Reported by Betty Evans

My grandfather, my dad, my brother and his son all shared the same name—William L. Valentine. My brother died when he was 29 years old. I was 18 at the time, and had seen my brother's son only once when he was four years old. Although I had thought of him often over the many years since his father's death, I didn't know where to find him. Sharing my sadness with God, I asked Him to help us find each other.

I had hoped that my nephew would want to find his birth family and would contact The Salvation Army to explore our family's roots. Then one day I received a phone call from The Salvation Army's Missing Persons Bureau in West Nyack, NY, reporting that a William L. Valentine III was inquiring about his family. In that moment I knew that my prayers had been answered!

My nephew, Bill, living in California, had visited the Missing Persons Bureau in San Diego, where he was advised to write to the territorial headquarters in West Nyack, NY. Within hours of receiving the news I spoke with him on the phone. Words couldn't describe my joy.

Reunion

My sister June and I were planning to bring our families together for a Valentine family reunion, despite her serious illness.

When Bill heard the news he booked a flight for the East Coast to meet us for the event.

Only 24 hours before the reunion, June died. Nevertheless, the reunion took place the next day with 37 family members in Kingston, NY. After we shared memories and offered each other comfort, we changed clothes and went to the funeral, conducted by my husband, Lt. Colonel Howard Evans of The Salvation Army. At the same time that we were holding our earthly reunion, we thought about June enjoying her own gathering with our mother, father, and brother on the other side.

> I hoped that my nephew would want to find his birth family and explore his roots.

Although saddened by the loss of my sister, I felt happy to have found my "lost Valentine." God had brought my whole family, and especially me, a renewed sense of His divine leading. I found this to be a giant step in my walk of faith with the Lord.

Lt. Colonel Betty Evans' story appeared in the War Cry. *She has retired from service in The Salvation Army.*

The Best Day Of My Life

Reported by Ruth Miller

W hen someone has cut off all contact, the worst part is in not knowing and allowing your imagination to run wild," Allen wrote to the Army's Missing Person's Bureau in West Nyack, NY. He and other family members were searching for his brother Tom.

"First of all I would like to thank you for your efforts on our behalf. I've just recently become aware of your service and since my father has already exhausted numerous other lines of inquiry, we hope you can help us. I'd like to provide additional details about my brother Tom."

Family History

"My family has no history of abuse or neglect. All four siblings had a happy and secure upbringing. I'm the oldest—eight years older than Tom. My sister Pearl lives in the South. My brother Sidney, who lives in Ohio, is also involved in this effort. Tom had a pattern of dropping out of sight for two or three months at a time, once going to Alaska without my parent's knowledge when he was a college student. All three of us are members of Alcoholics Anonymous, so it would not be surprising if Tom also shared this disease.

"The loss of our mother to cancer was the first experience of death in our immediate family. My own distress led me to presume that it was similarly devastating to Tom. My sister and I, in particular, share a strong tendency to 'deal through avoidance.' We've had extended periods of family estrangement that weren't the result of any overt conflict, but rather the isolative behavior endemic to people with substance abuse problems.

"Tom became a user of drugs and alcohol. In New York City, he was an advocate for tenants rights and a squatter in abandoned tenements. Through this experience, he may have learned how to live underground. He is quite artistic, majoring in journalism at the University of Mississippi, and his writings have been published in alternative publications.

"At times, at least three of us siblings have been isolated, and I know from personal experience that after a while estrangement can take on a life of its own—a vicious cycle fueled by guilt and shame. It's possible that Tom is caught in an extreme case of this, but we just don't know. I have children of my own and I'm in recovery. No matter what he thinks we're feeling, we'd be overjoyed to at least have knowledge of his whereabouts if not actual contact."

Joy And Gratitude

Four months later the Army received a follow-up letter from Allen. "It is with great joy and gratitude that I write to let you know that our "prodigal" brother and son has been located. Words can't even begin to describe what a miracle this has proven to be. My father had invested so much time and emotional energy in the search that he'd just about given up. He'd tried private detectives and numerous law enforcement agencies. To say he was overwhelmed by Tom's coming back into our lives would be a gross understatement!

> "Estrangement tends to take on a life of its own, fueled by guilt and shame."

"On a personal level this has been a great affirmation of faith and the power of prayer. I'd become somewhat discouraged when we didn't hear from Tom for a few months after contacting you. It turns out that his embarrassment and awkwardness over letting contact slip for so long had delayed his reply. I appreciate why his confidentiality had to be protected, and I'm thankful that he chose to write and let us know where he is. I've never been one to pray for a specific result—far be it from me to attempt to direct our Creator's will. It was simply 'Please God, if it is your will, please bring Tom back to us, but if that can't be, please take care of him.'

A West Coast Artist

"It turns out that he's living on the West Coast working as an artist. He's part owner of a business, and he has someone in his life whom he loves and who loves him. In fact, she helped nudge him into writing us. With a certain amount of chagrin, I recall images of him in far less happy circumstances. He's healthy and happy. Of course, he was afraid that we were mad at him. All of that flew out the window the moment I saw his name on the return address of the letter he sent. Things are better than I dared to hope.

"My other brother, who also lives here in Ohio, and I are going to meet him in Cleveland. My dad plans to fly out to California to see him.

"So you see, you really started something! Tom kept repeating on the phone, 'This is the best day of my life!' Thanks again from all of us. This has been a miracle! God bless you!"

A Change Of Heart

Reported by The Salvation Army's West Nyack, NY Office

T ony hadn't seen his mother, Alice, since his parents separated and he went to live with his father 28 years earlier.

He asked The Salvation Army to locate his maternal grandparents, who had also been estranged from Alice for many years. But his grandmother was unwilling to tell the Army the whereabouts of either her daughter or her grandson.

Questions

When Alice heard from relatives that Tony had been asking about her and his maternal relatives in England, she initiated her own search for him through The Salvation Army. Persistent, nagging questions often weighed her down: Will Tony want anything to do with me, after being abandoned so many years ago? Will he call me Mom if I am able to locate him? Did my husband turn our son against me? Will my mother help us to find each another? How will Tony feel about her now? What will he say?

A couple of letters from Tony to the Missing Persons Bureau helped to conclude the story. "I must apologize for taking so long in responding. As fate would have it, I recently heard from my mother this spring, and we are now in touch. As I understand it she went to you for help because my grandmother would not tell her of my whereabouts. Evidently my grandmother had a change of heart and this story may ultimately have a happy ending.

Thank–Yous

"I want to thank you for the good and valuable work The Salvation Army does in finding missing persons. Four years ago I began searching for my mother through your offices in England, and then got in touch with my grandmother. Despite her misgivings, it was my grandmother who gave my mother the idea to search for me through you. Anyhow, for my part, I thank you, and will remember your organization. God bless."

> ## "Did my husband turn our son against me?"

The Army also received a grateful letter from Alice:

"Thank you for your letter regarding my son Tony. I must apologize for being rather remiss in answering, but I think you'll understand that I've been very much preoccupied with making contact with him. I have, in fact, just returned from Canada where we met for the first time."

"We Felt We'd Always Known Each Other"

by Jørn Lauridsen

"There had always been a vacuum in my heart since I said good-bye to my child," Birgit said on meeting her son Erik for the first time in 48 years. Mother and son were overwhelmed as they hugged each other tightly beside the harbor just outside Copenhagen. Birgit's husband and Erik's wife, Vivian, and their two children, were on hand to witness this amazing moment.

Erik, an adopted child who grew up in a good home with loving parents, admitted that, "Not a single day has passed without my thinking of my mother." His adoptive parents had died when he was still young, leaving him alone in the world to finish his studies as a bank employee.

A Single Mother

Birgit had been raised in an affluent home in a small town in Denmark. Her father was a well-known citizen who ruled his family with an iron hand. Life was difficult in Denmark during the German occupation of World War II. Yet, despite the hardships, Birgit earned an apprenticeship as a dental technician. She met a much older man and became pregnant. "I was very naive, and I didn't even know where children came from," she explained, sounding a bit embarrassed.

Birgit felt trapped in an untenable situation. She even attempted to lose the baby, but despite her efforts she did not miscarry. At the end of the first trimester, she somehow found the courage to tell her mother that she was pregnant. Her mother so feared her father's reaction that she warned Birgit not to reveal the pregnancy to him.

Sent Away

Birgit's mother sent her to live in the nearby home of a midwife, where she scrubbed floors, washed clothes, sewed, tended the garden, and answered the telephone. Most of this time she was in tears. She caught only a glimpse of her newborn son before he was transferred to an infant home. A local businessman and his wife, who were residents of a nearby town, adopted him. They named him Erik after his biological father, who never even knew he had a son.

> She caught only a glimpse of her newborn son before they took him away.

Birgit then moved to Sweden, where she lived with her grandmother and learned a trade. After she married, she and her husband longed to find Erik, but they soon learned that she could not contact him legally. Erik had been adopted in Denmark, which meant that the search would have to wait until he tried to find his mother.

Search From Copenhagen

Then Erik and his wife Vivian, who lived in Copenhagen, initiated a search for Birgit through The Salvation Army. Erik learned that his mother was living in Sweden, and that she had tried unsuccessfully to trace him.

"When we met, we felt that we'd always known each other," they said spontaneously. Birgit was overjoyed with her new roles as mother, grandmother and mother-in-law.

Birgit and Erik

Colonel Jørn Lauridsen is the director of the Missing Persons Bureau in Copenhagen, Denmark.

"He Saved My Life"

Reported by Colin Fairclough

B rian was working on board a merchant ship that an-
chored at the port of East London in South Africa.
After he and several friends went ashore, they decided
to go for a swim to cool off. They were caught in a strong
undertow, and one member of the group drowned. Brian was
pulled to safety by a 15–year–old boy, and the account of his dramatic rescue was featured in a local newspaper.

Some years later, Brian's ship called again at the same port.
Going ashore to look for his shipmate's grave, he asked for direc-
tions to the cemetery. After a long walk, he found the cemetery, but
he couldn't locate the grave. Disappointed, he began making his
way back to the ship, which was due to sail shortly.

Chance Encounter

Outside the cemetery, he stopped an elderly man to inquire if
there was another burial ground in the city. Yes, he was told.
"Whose grave are you looking for?" asked the stranger. Brian re-
lated the tragic loss of his shipmate, and his good fortune to be res-
cued from the pounding surf by a young man from East London.
Then the stranger asked the name of his rescuer.

"David Brinton," replied Brian.

"He's my son," came the startling response. "At the moment he is away in college." Of all the people in town, Brian had sought help from the father of the man who had saved his life!

Almost 50 years after the accident, before leaving England on a trip to South Africa, Brian called The Salvation Army to initiate a search for David. He wanted to thank him for saving his life. Although this was a request that the Army ordinarily would not pursue, details were forwarded to the office in South Africa.

Ships In The Night

Two days before Brian was scheduled to depart, the Army notified him that David had been located and relayed his address and telephone number. Brian was elated at the prospect of meeting David, until he learned that David had moved from South Africa to Scotland!

> Brian had sought help from the father of the man who had saved his life!

Still, he took the time to call his rescuer before he left on his trip. In a letter to the Army he wrote, "You will never know what a burden has been lifted from my heart, to be able to thank the man who saved me from drowning, and who has so far given me an extra 48 years of life."

David and Brian finally met as a surprise reunion that was aired on a television program in which The Salvation Army took part.

A Mother's Quest

Reported by The Salvation Army's Chicago Office

F)or more than four decades, Mimi was on a quest to find a pair of smiling eyes.

She had been 18 years old, unmarried and living with her parents in Chicago when she discovered she was pregnant. Although she pleaded with her family to keep the child, they refused and her father took her to a Salvation Army Booth Hospital for single mothers. While there she was lovingly cared for and learned how to sew. Soon after her son's birth he was placed in an orphanage. Once a week, for almost two years, Mimi would sneak away to visit him until he was adopted.

She joined the U.S. Navy as a medic, served as a nurse in the Navy's medical corps during the Korean and Vietnam Wars, and received a purple heart.

But the void left by her only child always remained and she never stopped looking for him. Search after search came up empty. When she wrote a letter to the Booth Records Office telling her story, that inquiry seemed to be a dead end, too.

Around the same time a Salvation Army case manager heard a similar story from Lewis, a Texan who had been searching for his mother for more than 40 years. She tried to contact Mimi but her residence and name had changed.

After months of searching, mother and son were finally connected. When Lewis heard that his mother had been found, he grew

Once a week for two years, Mimi would sneak away to visit him until he was adopted.

as excited as a little kid. Initially they talked over the telephone, and then they met at a gas station in San Antonio, TX. Mimi had driven with her three dogs about 2,000 miles from Philadelphia to see her 62-year-old son. She and Lewis, a retired plant manager, trembled with excitement as they embraced each other for the first time.

Mimi learned that she had eight grandchildren and discovered that she and Lewis shared many mutual interests. They planned to build a house and live there together in Medina Lake, TX. Grateful to have found each other, they arrived at The Salvation Army for a visit, holding hands and wearing matching floral shirts that Mimi had made for them.

Pen Pals

Reported by Jørn Lauridsen

F ourteen–year–old Valerie could barely contain her excitement the day a Danish fishing boat docked near her home in New Zealand. Eleven fishermen had checked into The Salvation Army's guesthouse in New Plymouth Auckland, a lodging managed by her officer parents. Their visit brought a welcome diversion from Valerie's typical daily routine in the coastal town she called home. During their stay one of the fishermen, Aksel, asked Valerie if she would be a pen pal to his niece, Kirsten, back in Denmark.

Before he'd set sail, Kirsten had pleaded with her uncle to find someone with whom she could correspond in New Zealand. Valerie gladly agreed, and she and Kirsten wrote to each other faithfully for several years before eventually losing contact.

Time went by and both of the girls finished school and grew to adulthood. Valerie married, raised a family and became a grandmother. Yet the miles that separated them and the difference in culture were not enough to break the strong bond of friendship.

Now a senior citizen, Valerie decided to write to The Salvation Army in Denmark and request a search for Kirsten, who lived more than 10,000 miles away. She wanted her old friend to know that she remembered her fondly and hoped she was well and happy. She'd saved all of her letters and photos as precious mementos of the special relationship they had shared as teenagers.

The miles that separated them were not enough to break the strong bond of friendship.

Valerie ended her letter by describing her daily routine with friends and family. She wrote about playing the piano at a Salvation Army corps in New Plymouth, adding that she was nearly blind and losing her spatial orientation. Anxious to hear from Kirsten, she felt that time might be running out for her.

The Missing Persons Bureau in Denmark managed to trace Kirsten through an old address and informed her of Valerie's desire to reach her again. Although the focus of their letters would no doubt change, the deep connection they had established as adolescents would remain as strong as ever now that they were back in contact.

"Find Bill"

Reported by Meta L. Maxwell

W hen my older brother Bill vanished from home, I was in my teens and he was 38 years old.

My parents hired private detectives to find him, to no avail. All I had to remember him by was a doll that he had sent me while he was stationed with the Air Force in Germany. For years, when I looked at the pretty doll with its long blonde braids, lace blouse and black pinafore, I wished we could be together.

My father died and the following year my mother had a heart attack while I was working in Bombay, India. She was in her seventies, and I feared I would soon lose her, too. I resigned from my job and moved to Eugene, OR, to be with her. What she wanted most of all, she said, was to "find Bill."

Far And Wide

I traveled to Sacramento to begin my search, meeting with homicide detectives, prowling the missions in the area, and hanging posters with his picture. Mother and I had all but given up hope of ever finding Bill, fearing that most likely he was dead.

Years passed with my mother looking into the face of every man on the street to see if he was her son. I pursued a new career, found new friends, and tried unsuccessfully to fill the place in my heart reserved for my brother.

My hopes of finding him were revived when I read a "Dear Abby" column in a daily newspaper, explaining how The Salvation Army could help find missing people. I called the Army, obtained the address for the Missing Persons Bureau and immediately submitted a letter with Bill's date and place of birth, Social Security number, last known address, the reason why he was missing and why we wanted desperately to find him.

> ## Bill had been hit by a truck and needed extensive surgery and rehabilitation.

Two years later, a caseworker called to tell me that the Army had found Bill and that he was alive, but she couldn't tell me where he was yet. She asked me if we still wanted to find him. Of course we did! She told me to stay by the phone and that if he wanted to talk with us, she would have him call.

Minutes later we were reunited by phone.

"Billy, this is your sister Meta," I choked through tears.

"Oh, hi Meta," he said.

"Mom's here too," I told him. "Would you like to talk with her?"

"Sure," he replied.

After learning that Bill was living in a home for veterans in California. we threw what we needed into the car and headed south to see him.

The next day was one of the best days of my life. Amazingly, it felt as if no time had passed since we last met, and we immediately resumed a loving relationship.

The Accident

Years earlier Bill had been hit by a truck while crossing the street, sustaining serious injuries that required extensive surgery and rehabilitation. He had no personal identification with him and could not contact his family. While he was recuperating in the hospital, one of his doctors took a special interest in him. Recognizing that Bill couldn't live independently, this doctor kindly escorted him to Sacramento and arranged for him to live in a home for veterans.

During all those years that Mom and I were worrying about Bill, the staff at the veterans' home had been taking good care of him. He had a safe, clean place to live, good meals, health care and a job in the library that fit his physical and mental abilities. He also had companionship with more than 1,200 other veterans who, in many cases, now served as each other's family.

I see Bill frequently now, taking him on vacations and bringing him home to visit and share family events. We enjoy talking about books, watching movies, eating, playing chess and just being together.

My eternal thanks go to The Salvation Army's Missing Persons Bureau for the peace and joy they delivered when they reunited us with Bill. May their work never cease and may the blessings they give return to them manyfold.

Meta with her brother, Bill

Meta Maxwell's story appeared in the War Cry.

The Birthstone

Reported by The Salvation Army's Chicago Office

Keepsakes can provide a powerful way of connecting us to people who are missing from our lives. They typically hold meaning solely for the one who cherishes them, until that person dies and family members come to understand why they were so treasured.

Shirley was a retired nurse and widow facing cancer surgery, the mother of six married children who lived nearby. A loving couple who later added two more children to their family had adopted her. At age 73, Shirley assumed that her birth mother, Mildred, had died, but she wondered if she had any siblings. She'd always hoped to find a sister.

When Mildred became pregnant with Shirley, she was living with her parents and two daughters from her first marriage. Her parents were supporting all of them and another baby was more than they could care for. They tried to keep her, but when Shirley was 18 months old, they put her up for adoption. Mildred later re-married and had a fourth child.

One Child Left

Only one of the four children, Lorraine, was still alive. When The Salvation Army Missing Persons Bureau contacted her, they learned that Mildred had indeed, died. Lorraine didn't know about

Shirley, but she said, "I always had a feeling my mother was keeping something back from me. I wish she had told me."

Lorraine was 68 years old, and like Shirley, a retired nurse. Although a resident of Florida, she'd been staying in Milwaukee with her daughter who was facing cancer surgery. Lorraine would also be having cancer surgery there. Since Shirley lived in Wisconsin, they were able to meet almost immediately. Shirley and her daughter traveled to Oak Creek, WI, to visit Lorraine.

Ironically, the two Salvation Army officials assigned to the case also traveled to Oak Creek to discuss their work at the Booth Hospital Records Office. Even more surprisingly, they discovered that Shirley and her daughter were members of the audience. Lorraine could not attend the gathering because she was recuperating from surgery.

> "I always had a feeling my mother was keeping something back from me."

Shirley freely shared her testimony with the group, proudly displaying a ring from her birth mother that Lorraine had given her. Lorraine always wondered why her mother wore this ring, since the stone didn't represent the birthday of anyone in the family. It didn't surprise her to learn that the stone in the ring was Shirley's birthstone. Shirley now treasures this ring.

"It's never too late to hope," she said. "God does answer prayer."

A 60 Year Old Secret

Reported by the War Cry in the United Kingdom

A childless couple, having answered a newspaper advertisement, waits with open arms to receive a baby at a railway station in England. They plan to welcome the six-week-old boy as their own, rename him, and give him the best life possible. This story resonates like a Dickens novel set against the backdrop of an impoverished family in Victorian England.

Actually, the shadowy exchange of this infant took place at a time when people everywhere hungered for the latest war news from Europe and Japan. For 60 years the handover remained a closely guarded family secret—until Dave asked The Salvation Army's Family Tracing Service to research his background. The Army located his brother—prize-winning author Ian McEwan—along with his half-brother and half-sister.

The Catalyst

"Becoming a grandparent was the catalyst for my search," Dave says thoughtfully. "I wanted to write something about my life and family history for my grandson to read when he was older. I'd known since the age of 14 that Percy and Rose—the people I called Mom and Dad—weren't my biological parents. They didn't tell me that until I needed my birth certificate for insurance purposes when I left school.

"The certificate listed my parents as Ernest and Rose, and my name as Stewart David—not David Stuart. Mom and Dad assured me that they loved me as their own, but they were upset, so I didn't ask any more questions. I felt badly, and we never mentioned it again."

When Dave became engaged, he worried about his fiancée Julie's reaction to his parentage. His future father-in-law advised him to legally change his name to Sharp, which he did.

"Mom and Dad were as pleased as punch, and when I told Julie they weren't my birth parents, she told me that *she* was adopted. I couldn't believe it." After Rose died of cancer, Dave, then about 20 years old, started to feel comfortable seeking information about his heritage.

"'One night I asked Dad how he and Mom had adopted me. He was reluctant to answer, but I gently pointed out that I had a right to know. Then he blurted out: 'We got you from a newspaper ad.'

"That's all he would say. And suddenly I had this picture in my mind of a baby wrapped up in a newspaper, like fish and chips!"

An Advertisement

Dave's next step was to comb the archives at the public library. Eventually he ran across an advertisement in the personal column of the local newspaper: "Wanted – Home for baby boy, age one month; complete surrender."

Dave knew that the baby had to be him. All of the dates fit, and the secrecy made sense as well.

"My adoptive parents had reversed my first and middle name and changed the spelling, perhaps to make me more their own, or maybe to protect my identity. Naturally I wanted to know why I had been given away and whether I had brothers and sisters, but I decided that any future searching must be done secretly to avoid upsetting Dad," Dave said.

"I couldn't have asked for a kinder father. We didn't have much money, but I never went without anything," he said.

After Dave married Julie, work and family took up most of his time and energy, and the search for his roots was temporarily put on hold. Five years later, he obtained his full birth certificate, which confirmed the names and address of his birth parents.

Percy died, leaving Dave wondering if he would ever know the truth about his birth. It took the arrival of his own grandson to spur him into action. He placed a newspaper advertisement asking for information about his birth parents. There were no replies.

Making Headway

Then he succeeded in finding a woman named Kathleen, who had been a tenant of the Sharp family. She referred him to The Salvation Army. Dave provided birth certificates and copies of the newspaper advertisements and waited.

About ten weeks later a letter from the Army arrived, reporting that some of his relatives had been found. A second letter revealed that a son and daughter, also born to Ernest and Rose, had known nothing of Dave's existence. Rose, meanwhile, had remarried after the war and had given birth to another son.

"I was so excited," Dave recalled. "I called the Missing Persons Bureau with dozens of questions. Apparently I had come as a shock to the rest of my family, and they needed time to get used to the idea. I had to be patient. It was now up to the family to decide if they wanted to respond further. He suggested I write to them through The Salvation Army, which I did."

> "Wanted - Home for baby boy, age one month."

Meeting Ian

A reply came from someone who introduced himself as Dave's "full" brother—author Ian McEwan, author of the critically acclaimed novel, *Atonement*. Ian was the son of Rose and her second husband, Sergeant-Major David McEwan, who was also the father of Dave. Rose, now in her eighties, was living in a nursing home with dementia. Her two other children were Dave's half-brother and half-sister.

Ian confirmed that he and his siblings had known nothing of Dave's existence, or the newspaper advertisement, before the letter arrived from the Army. He and Dave met for the first time in the lobby of a hotel.

"We talked for three hours and discovered we lived totally different lives," Dave said. "I'm a bricklayer, he's a famous author; I love football, he doesn't!"

A Sworn Promise

Ian managed to shed some light on the burning question: Why had Dave been given away? When the family had met to discuss Dave's letter, Rose's sister, Margie, made an extraordinary confession. For 60 years she had kept a sworn promise to her sister never to reveal what had happened that day at Reading Station.

Dave explained: "While her husband Ernest was away fighting in North Africa, Rose had a relationship with David McEwan and became pregnant. I was born and given the name Stewart. Then Ernest returned home on leave and the drastic decision was made to run a newspaper advertisement seeking a home for me.

"Percy and Rose were the first to reply. Other couples who wrote in to the P.O. Box number were kept "on file" in case Percy and Rose changed their minds before the handover occurred.

The Adoption

"A date was set, and Rose and her sister took me by train about 20 miles away. Apparently I screamed all the way. Rose, Margie, and the Sharps had agreed to wait until everyone else left the platform before making contact. Rose then handed me over with a bag of clothes and a birth certificate falsely naming her husband as my father—and that was that. She got rid of her problem, and the Sharps got what they wanted—a child.

"In those days, having an affair with a married woman while her husband was away at war would have meant a court martial and almost certainly the end of David McEwan's military career. It would have been impossible to keep the relationship secret in the small village where Rose lived. She would have been disgraced, and I would have been branded as illegitimate."

To further maintain the secrecy, Rose also sent her two older children away—the boy to his grandparents, and the girl to a military orphanage. Ernest, meanwhile, died as a result of wounds during the D-Day invasion of Normandy. After his death, David and Rose married and had a second son, Ian. Because David refused to let Rose's other children live with them, they grew up away from their mother just as Dave did.

Ian's Insight

Ian's understanding of his father helped Dave to absorb what had happened. "He studied the newspaper advertisement closely, and he thinks our father's fingerprints are all over it. He was a hard, dominant man with no love in him. If you wanted a good home for a puppy, you would at least write 'loving home wanted.' It makes me sound like an unwanted pet – and 'complete surrender' is a military term."

Dave was reunited with his birth mother on Mother's Day. "I felt like a kid on Christmas morning—she was still my mother, even though she'd given me away," he said. "I hoped that she had some memory left despite the dementia, and I asked her how many children she had. She said five, and then she quickly reeled off the names of her caregivers in the nursing home.

"I had no feelings towards her, and I felt guilty about letting the Sharps down. They'd taken me in and cared for me as their own son. I certainly wouldn't have done the search if they'd been alive," he said.

Telling His Story

Dave visited Rose several times before her death later that same year.

He has written a book about this experience, *Complete Surrender,* and brother Ian contributed the foreword. Is he sure of his identity now?

"I don't feel any different. The taxman says that I'm Dave Sharp, and that's who I answer to! My mom and dad are the ones who brought me up and shaped me into what I am. I suppose I could have been given to someone evil, but instead fortune—or God—smiled on me, and sent me two lovely parents.

"Finding out about my family has been an emotional roller coaster. Now I know the answers to those nagging questions and can draw a line under the extraordinary events of my early life. Before she died, my birth mother told her caregivers that she had once lost a child. Perhaps something had penetrated the haze of dementia after all. But I wasn't really lost—just mislaid for a while."

The Confidant

Reported by The Salvation Army's Chicago Office

O ften an older sibling will help take care of younger brothers and sisters, especially in a large family. But sometimes the sibling will shoulder as much responsibility as a parent. The loss of a child can be very devastating to the older sibling who has cared for him. A case in point involved Patricia, who was a high-school student when her brother Larry was born.

After her parents divorced, 16-year-old Patricia took primary responsibility for her six siblings and for running the family household. Shortly after the divorce, her mother, Edna, discovered she was pregnant again. Edna took the train from Michigan to Kentucky to request child support from her husband, but he refused to give her any financial help. Under the circumstances, she decided to place Larry up for adoption. She took Patricia into her confidence.

Patricia went to the hospital with Edna when Larry was born, and she was there when his adoptive family came to pick him up. Her mother told her to forget about the baby. Never tell anyone about him and never mention him again, she told her daughter.

Edna remained at The Salvation Army's Booth Hospital for three months, leaving Patricia to care for the home and her other siblings. Family and friends were told that Edna had suffered a nervous breakdown.

Patricia never mentioned her brother to her mother again, but she never forgot him. After Edna died she began to search for Larry in earnest.

For 10 years, Patricia tried to find Larry on her own, but every avenue seemed to lead to a dead end. Then she called The Salvation Army, and within an hour, a county agency had put her in touch with Larry's adoptive mother. She learned that her brother had been a perfect student who was blessed with musical talent. He had grown up on a large fruit farm in Michigan as the center of his parent's universe. Then a tour of Vietnam turned his life upside down. He began drinking and using drugs, drifted to Arizona, and stopped communicating with his family. A few years later he died.

> "Never tell anyone and never mention him again."

Although this story left Patricia heartbroken, at the same time she felt great peace after talking to the woman who had loved him and cared for him. She traveled all the way from Alaska to Michigan to meet his family, and she saw pictures of her brother when he was growing up. Reminiscing with his family gave her a chance to know Larry and to fill the void his absence had left in her life. She felt grateful that God had given him loving parents who did their best for him.

"Utterly Amazed"

Reported by Colin Fairclough

R osemary learned from her brother in Australia that another brother, Frank, was homeless in Los Angeles. The police had contacted him about Frank, but he was nearing retirement and not in a position to help out financially.

Since Frank had left England about 40 years earlier, he failed to qualify for a pension or any other government benefits. Given his financial situation, Rosemary asked The Salvation Army to find him and help take care of him. Her only point of contact was the police department in Los Angeles.

The Salvation Army wrote to the police in California, but their brief contact with Frank had ceased, and they had no clue what had become of him. After a three-year search, the Missing Persons Bureau had to admit defeat.

A Long Shot

In England, the Army made a few tentative inquiries, despite the fact that Frank had been out of touch for so long. Then a telephone call came from a hospital in Cambridge, England, indicating that a patient there seemed to match Frank's description. On a long shot, Rosemary went to the hospital to see if this man was really her brother. She wrote to say that the patient she had visited actually was Frank, whom she had not seen for nearly 45 years. Although

> **"I am utterly amazed that he should be found not three miles from my home."**

he was in poor mental health, he was able to recognize photographs of other relatives shown to him by his sister.

In a remarkable coincidence, a Good Samaritan in the United States had generously offered to cover the cost of Frank's transatlantic airfare. On his arrival in England he had been taken to the hospital in Cambridge, where Rosemary was living!

Rosemary wrote, "I am utterly amazed that he was found not three miles from my home, when I had thought he was in Los Angeles. Although I don't pretend to be a religious person, I'm sure God has sent him to Cambridge so that I can love and care for him."

Rosemary and Frank

Where's Ishmael?

Reported by the Wednesday Journal of Oak Park and River Forest, IL

N icolasa left her husband in Dallas, TX, to help her sister operate a restaurant in Fargo, ND. A year later she died.

Her six children then headed for Mason City, IA—where five sons were to live with a family friend, and a daughter, Luz, with an aunt. Along the way, they left baby Ishmael in Mankato, MI, promising to return for him the next week. But they didn't go back.

Ishmael went to live with a childless couple who never told him that he had been adopted. When memories of his siblings troubled him, his foster father insisted that they were his cousins. Years later he learned of his true heritage when he was unable to obtain a birth certificate. Baptismal records from the Catholic Church revealed that he had been christened under the name Ramirez.

Meanwhile, the other children had returned to Dallas to live with their father, Juan. Immediately the family began looking for Ishmael, but the trail was cold.

Many years later Ishmael began to search in earnest for his brothers and sister. He had lost his sight, was receiving dialysis to treat diabetes, and wanted to find his family before he died. A book on locating families led him to The Salvation Army's Missing Persons Bureau. He gave the Army all the information he had collected and waited for a response.

One of the brothers, Camerino, received a letter saying that Ishmael wanted to contact him, and then the family scheduled a reunion at Ishmael's home in Chicago. Camerino and Ernesto came from Texas. None of them had seen each other in 60 years.

> ## They left baby Ishmael in Minnesota and didn't go back for him.

The brothers' physical resemblance was unmistakable—all three had almond-shaped eyes, bushy eyebrows, and faces young enough to make people doubt their real ages. Ishmael had developed a hard-edged Chicago accent, while his brothers spoke in a soft Texas twang.

Camerino lamented all of the years he had spent searching for Ishmael. "We looked, but we couldn't find him," he said sadly. "So we just suffered and suffered. Now I can rest, because the whole family couldn't rest these past 60 years."

What if Ishmael's foster parents had told him he was adopted? What if either side had known the other's last name? With 60 years to catch up on, the brothers agreed that it was pointless to spend their reunion dwelling on what might have been.

Who Am I?

Reported by Colin Fairclough

S ylvia, filled with despair, completed the missing persons questionnaire by describing the person she wanted to trace as "myself." She had little information that would help The Salvation Army to pursue her case.

A Dreadful Start

The woman she believed to be her mother had married at the age of 15, and had separated from her husband less than three years later. She then worked as a housekeeper for a man by whom she had two children. After a letter from the National Children's Home, a well-known charity in the United Kingdom, described her living conditions as "appallingly bad," her four-month-old daughter, Sylvia, was placed in an orphanage suffering from malnutrition.

At the age of four, Sylvia went to live with a foster family. She couldn't speak, and she drank from a baby bottle. A year later, her foster mother had thyroid surgery, which changed her temperament dramatically.

"From the age of five," Sylvia said, "my life was pure hell. I was beaten and made to work. I sawed wood, broke up coal, and cleaned the house. I was treated like a slave. I couldn't read, and my speech was all jumbled up."

Although her foster mother abused her, her foster father, who was scared of his wife, treated her kindly. He died when Sylvia was

13 years old. Her foster mother blamed her for his death and forced her to view his dead body. Every day she was made to feel that somehow she had killed the only person who had shown her any love. At the age of 14, she attempted suicide, but she was rushed to the emergency room and doctors there revived her. She still couldn't read or write.

The National Children's Home found her a job as a nanny. Then her birth mother arrived on the scene, taking her back simply because she was old enough to work. "My mother was promiscuous," she said. "The house was dirty and she didn't want me. She always told me that I wasn't her child. Even my grandfather told me this. I ran away once, and the police brought me back. After a year, my mother kicked me out. When I came home one day, my bags were packed, and she told me to leave."

More Heartbreak

At the age of 21, Sylvia fell in love and married. She gave birth to a healthy baby boy, but later she had a daughter who was born with a major birth defect. The child died before her third birthday. A year later, Sylvia tried to commit suicide a second time, and again she was rushed to the hospital in the nick of time. Her eldest son became diabetic, and a second son was diagnosed with cancer of the hip. Sylvia's marriage broke up after 20 years.

> Robert was thrilled to learn that his "baby sister" was looking for him.

In her late thirties, she finally learned how to read and write. Several years later she asked The Salvation Army to establish the true identity of her birth mother and to determine whether she was still alive. Rather than look for her birth mother, the Army agreed to search for possible siblings, hoping that this would give her a new direction in life at the age of 50.

Finding Robert

It didn't take long to locate her brother, Robert, who was two years older than Sylvia. He had been born to her mother and the man for whom she had worked as housekeeper. Robert was thrilled to learn that his "baby sister" was looking for him. Sylvia said, "I can't express in words how I felt the moment we saw each other. It was as if time had stopped for both of us." Robert told her that their mother had died about seven years earlier, which meant that Sylvia would never know why her mother had denied that she was her child.

Hope

As the Army's role in the case neared an end, Sylvia was preparing to re-marry, rejoicing that this time her brother would attend her wedding.

Amazingly, this woman who had been abused and illiterate well into adulthood discovered a gift for words, and she began to write short stories for children and adults. After all the heartbreak Sylvia had endured, it looked as though she would finally have a chance to experience real joy. She was, after all, a true survivor who never gave up hope.

The Treasure Of Friendship

Reported by The Salvation Army's Chicago Office

T rue friends are hard to find, and when we do, we treasure them and never let them go.

Gertrude and Doreen had been friends for so long that it was hard to remember a time when they weren't part of each other's lives. As they grew older, however, their lives began to change. Gertrude, in her late 70's, moved in with her daughter Dawn. When Dawn moved from Detroit, MI, to Illinois, Gertrude joined her. But her relationship with Doreen continued to thrive through visits, phone calls and letters.

As Gertrude's health worsened, she couldn't make the trip to see Doreen as often as she would have liked. One day, Gertrude discovered that Doreen's phone number had been disconnected, and she feared that something was terribly wrong. Dawn drove her to Detroit, they knocked on the front door, and there was no answer. The house looked empty and next-door neighbors hadn't seen Doreen in a while. They thought that she had gotten sick and moved away, but they didn't know for sure.

Gertrude was distraught. What if Doreen needed her? How would she find her? She and Dawn contacted all of the hospitals and nursing homes in the vicinity trying to locate Doreen's family members. They called the police, the Red Cross, and then they called The Salvation Army. Dawn explained that although

> Gertrude feared that something was terribly wrong.

Gertrude and Doreen were friends, not relatives, they had nowhere else to turn for help. Gertrude was getting weaker and weaker, weighed down with worry over Doreen.

The Salvation Army found a trail of addresses, starting from Doreen's empty house to another address in Detroit and finally one in South Carolina. The Missing Persons Bureau wrote to the address in South Carolina, but there was no response. Repeated calls were also made until one day Doreen finally answered the phone. The caseworker asked some key questions to make sure she had the right person. She was puzzled by the answers.

"Do you have a friend named Gertrude?"

"I don't know."

"Were you a nurse?"

"I think so."

"Do you know anyone named Dawn?"

"I think she's my friend's daughter."

Finally, a connection! Doreen explained that she didn't remember much, but she was living with her niece who would be home after work. Rather than have the niece call Gertrude, the caseworker urged Doreen to call in the hope that hearing her friend's voice would jog her memory.

Doreen was suffering from rapidly progressing dementia. Talking with Gertrude helped her to recall bits and pieces of their friendship. Gertrude continued to call her and write to her, even though most days Doreen didn't know who she was. Dawn told the Salvation Army that since finding Doreen, her mother's health had greatly improved. Her frailty was gone and her strength had been restored.

An Eternal Embrace

Reported by Dawn Chavez

T) ears streaming down our faces, my friend Cindy and I prayed for God's strength as she grieved the loss of her birth father. She had never met him and now could know him only through the memories of others.

As I prayed for Cindy I thought about Dawn, my beautiful baby girl who was born less than two weeks after my 16th birthday. Could she be looking for me? Could she be in such pain? God had used my friend's faith to melt away my shame and guilt, allowing me to see my 25–year–old secret in a different light.

When I called The Salvation Army, loving and encouraging people greeted me. A flood of emotions surged through me as I remembered the difficult decision to give her up. Would I find her? Would she want to see me? Did I have any right to burst into her life?

I decided to be patient and see what God had in store for me. Comforting words from the Old Testament prophet Joel strengthened me while I waited for an answer.

Weeks later The Salvation Army called to say that my daughter was trying to contact me. Several hours passed, and my heart stopped every time the phone rang.

Finally my daughter called and I heard the sweetest voice say, "Dawn? This is Susan." We arranged to meet the next morning at

> "A flood of emotions passed through me as I remembered the difficult decision to give up my daughter."

my house. My heart overflowed when Susan said she would bring along my grandson, one-year-old Adam.

At 9:00 a.m. the next day my 19-year-old daughter, Mari, screamed, "Mom, they're here!" My husband, T.J., opened Susan's car door and I buried my head in her shoulder, holding on as tightly as I could. Our embrace seemed eternal. We were caught up in a timeless love. I knew that God had opened both our hearts for restoration. When we finally looked at each other, she was breathtaking, so unique yet so much like me.

We're proud to be a family. God has given us a miracle.

Dawn, Debra Lewis (former missing persons director in Chicago) and Susan

Dawn Chavez's story appeared in The Salvation Army's Central News.

Joy Poured Out

Reported by The Salvation Army's Chicago Office

"**I**'m writing to thank you for your help in reuniting me with my brother Steven. I should have written a lot sooner, but to be honest, I was in shock and I wanted to see how things would go. I'm very happy to tell you that since our first conversation—which was the very day I spoke to Steven—we have talked for hours. I discovered that I'm an aunt to three wonderful little girls as well as a sister-in-law to a kind, sincere woman. I've met part of my family that I didn't even know I had and just can't put into words how excited and happy I am.

"I can't believe that for the past 10 years I've wondered how Steven was. I didn't know if he was safe or even if he was alive, and I had no idea that he lived so close to me! To learn that he was safe and well brought me peace of mind, and that was all I had asked for.

"I'm thrilled to say that I found more than that . . . not only are we talking like we were never separated, but we get along well and I love his entire family. As I write this note a lot of emotions are fluttering around inside me. It's strange and new not to have to wonder about how or where Steven is. I'm so used to that uncomfortable wonder. Now all that stress has vanished with just one phone call!

"Because of your help and kindness, I no longer have to tell friends that I have a brother *somewhere* out there. Thank you for all

> "It's strange not to have to wonder about how or where Steven is."

of your work and for speaking with Steven personally. He said you were very nice and helpful and showed real concern in making sure he understood everything. You expressed genuine interest in his plans and you took the time to read my message to him. That's why I'm happy to send you this letter. You have brought unexpected happiness to at least a dozen people. So I send a million thank–yous. I try not to take kind people for granted, so I wish you the very, very best."

Forgiven

Reported by Ruth Miller

W ithout you, I would never have known how much my family loves me. I feel a great peace along with sadness that my dad is gone," Gloria wrote to The Salvation Army. She had a poignant reunion with her siblings and the chance to say goodbye to her father before he died.

"You helped my sister Jane to locate me and to resume contact a couple of years ago. I wanted to tell you all what you did for us."

An Ill Father

"Because my sister contacted you, she was able to let me know that our father was very ill, and I traveled to Rochester, NY, to see him for the first time in 12 years. It was hard, but I feel very blessed in that he knew I was his missing daughter who had returned. He also let me know that he still loved me, and I was able to tell him that I'm all right and have married a wonderful man. During my visit, I saw my mother and my older sister, neither of whom I'd seen in a very long time. There were lots of tears and hugs.

"Last week Dad suddenly took a real turn for the worse. Jane informed me and also let me know that he had died Wednesday night. My husband and I attended the wake, and it was amazing to me how many lives my father had touched. The room was full of people, and there was much laughter mixed with grief—because it isn't possible to talk about my father without remembering something funny he said or did in his lifetime.

Reconnecting

"At one point while I was waiting to speak with someone, I felt my arm grabbed and I was whirled around and enveloped in a wonderful hug. Looking up, I realized that it was my big brother Mark. Although he's six years older than I am, we'd been quite close because our busy mother used to choose one sibling to watch out for a younger child and I was his 'assignment.' He told me that night, with tears in his eyes, that it hurt when I left, that he loved me, that he was sorry for all the things that had happened to me when I was young, and that he wanted me never to leave again.

> ## I felt my arm grabbed and I was whirled around and enveloped in a wonderful hug.

"My aunt said that my father had asked her if she knew where I was about 10 years ago. I was so afraid because I knew that I had done some terribly hurtful things to my family—things I thought were unforgiveable. Over the years there had been other breaks within our family. The illness and loss of our father seems to have healed an awful lot of that, though. The funeral was both sad and joyful."

Realistic Expectations

Reported by The Salvation Army's Chicago Office

"**I** want to extend our thanks and gratitude to all of you who helped me find my brother. After you located him for us, we sent him clothing, phone cards, personal items, and money. We talked with him on the phone constantly and did whatever we could do to help. We arranged temporary housing, but all of our love and efforts weren't enough as John continued in the alcoholism that has been his way of life for so long.

"I traveled to Colorado to see him and to represent the rest of the family. I could write a book on our experiences. We have learned a lot. Mostly, however, we've learned that you can't change someone, no matter how much you want to.

"John is doing so much better since I went to visit him. I think we've all grown from this experience, and we've learned to be more realistic about our expectations. He's beginning to realize that we love him even through these difficult times and the downward spirals in his life. He's now met a registered nurse through one of the rehabilitation programs and she's been like his 'angel.' They both have their own problems, but they are together now and trying to survive.

"Every day on my way to and from work, I see the lost souls, the human beings who have given up . . . the homeless, the handi-

> "We've learned that you can't change someone, no matter how much you want to."

capped, the abused who are ignored in body, mind and spirit. Seeing them reminds me of my brother, John, and the miracle it is to have him back in our lives. Circumstances are still difficult and he struggles daily with demons we'll never know about, but there is hope.

"We're so grateful to have contact with John and we continue all possible efforts to help him get back on his feet. It has brought my mother and the rest of us comfort to know that he is alive, and that we can support him. We have to leave so much to God and his loving care. It is with my family's sincere thanks and gratitude that we send our prayers for your good works. Without your help, our family would still be in the depths of despair without any hope."

Following A Dream

Reported by Veronica Trollip

E ver since he'd seen Marlin Brando as Terry Malloy in "On the Waterfront," 20-year-old Jurgen had longed to be an actor. Not just a movie star, but a strong, dramatic character actor. With or without the support of his family, he resolved to follow his lifelong dream. On a trip to South Africa, he was elated to land the role of the gentleman caller in Tennessee Williams' "The Glass Menagerie." Johannesburg was a long way from his home in Stuttgart, but this could be the big career break he had been waiting for. Always the free spirit, he decided he had nothing to lose.

The play was a hit, and he was encouraged by his performance. After it ended, though, no other part was waiting in the wings, and Jurgen had no Plan B. He began working part-time as a waiter while continuing to audition for other parts in the theater. But after he arrived late to work one time too many, the manager of the restaurant decided to let him go. His bank account was nearly overdrawn, and he began to feel desperate.

He anticipated the response he would receive if he called home, because his parents had always wanted him to pursue a more traditional career, like law or business. It was all he could do to swallow his pride and ask his father for financial help.

"Get a decent job," his father said angrily, and he hung up the phone. Shortly thereafter, Jurgen's parents lost all contact with him.

But his mother had a soft spot for her youngest son. Like Jurgen, she had always been somewhat of a romantic. After she and her husband moved to Greece, she contacted The Salvation Army's Missing Persons Bureau and initiated a search for him. She gave the Army the names of two of his friends, but they had no idea where he was living. A year went by, and still no trace of Jurgen.

> Jurgen had been spotted sleeping in the doorway of a nearby shop.

Then, one rainy winter evening the phone rang at The Salvation Army office in Johannesburg. The caller had spotted him sleeping in the doorway of a nearby shop. Acting on this reliable tip, a Salvation Army officer, who visited this neighborhood just before midnight, gently lifted the blanket of every homeless person, hoping to uncover Jurgen. But he was nowhere to be found.

Then the Army officer met a security guard assigned to the area who knew him. The guard promised to let Jurgen know that The Salvation Army was searching for him. One week later, when the hopeful officer returned to the area, the guard announced happily, "Here he comes now!"

Astonished to learn that his parents were looking for him, Jurgen repeated the last conversation he had had with his father. The Army officer assured him that his father had spoken in the heat of the moment, and that he sorely regretted his harsh words. Jurgen's parents boarded the next flight to South Africa to bring him home.

Lt. Colonel Veronica Trollip is the director of the Family Tracing Service in Johannesburg, South Africa. Her story appeared in the War Cry *in South Africa.*

Two Sonny Rays

Reported by Betty Anderson

W hen the person initiating a search has the same name as the person who is missing, investigations can get pretty confusing for Salvation Army caseworkers. They start to feel like emcees on the long-running television game show, *To Tell the Truth*, where all the contestants simultaneously stood up and claimed to be the same individual. It was up to a panel of celebrities, through a series of probing questions, to single out the "real" contestant from those who were impersonators.

One transatlantic missing persons case involved two men, each with the same name, born to the same father but different mothers.

In Stockholm, Sonny Ray contacted The Salvation Army's Missing Persons Bureau in search of his half-brother. His father was a Swedish immigrant, and his mother was Norwegian. After their divorce, his father was deported because of his role as a union organizer, and then he returned to Sweden. Sonny Ray remained with his mother in the United States. Back in Sweden, his father remarried and his second wife gave birth to his second son, whom they also named Sonny Ray.

The Swedish Sonny Ray initiated a search for his American brother, who by then was 76 years old. During the course of its research, The Missing Persons Bureau in West Nyack, NY, discovered that the Sonny Ray in America had died.

Sonny Ray was deported because of his role as a union organizer.

Through an odd coincidence, the Bureau also found that he had a relative named Audrey, a Salvation Army officer who had retired in Spokane, WA. Audrey and her sister Violet began to correspond with Sonny Ray, now living in a small town near the Arctic Circle in Sweden. He belonged to a male chorus that had scheduled a four-city tour of the United States.

He asked if Audrey and Violet would be interested in getting together with him. The answer came back a definitive yes, and he and his wife, Gunilla, had a long-delayed reunion with his cousins in Olympia, WA.

SHORT STORIES AND THANK-YOUS

Perfect Timing

Reported by Debra Lewis

Kelly cherished the extraordinary love her parents had felt for each other.

Patricia was a college student and Tommy, a Hungarian immigrant, was learning how to make his way in America. When Patricia became pregnant, she moved back in with her parents because she and Tommy couldn't support a family together. Although they wanted to marry, her parents ordered him to leave and never come back. Eventually, Patricia married a friend of the family.

Tommy saw baby Kelly on several occasions, but when Patricia started to have marital problems, she severed contact with him. Kelly didn't know Tommy was her father until she was 15 years old. That year he began a Salvation Army search for her, to no avail.

After Kelly married and had children, she began to wonder about her father. She scoured the Internet and made many telephone calls to locate him, but her efforts always seemed to hit a dead end. She prayed desperately for help.

Meanwhile, Tommy's son, Kelly's half-brother, decided to pick up the trail where his father had left off. Soon she received a call from him. "It was God's timing," she said. "The day he called was my father's birthday."

Although Tommy had already died, Kelly was eager to meet his family. Unable to afford the plane fare, she prayed for a solution to her problem. Then a friend handed her mother a check for the exact amount that her flight would cost. "Something told me to give you this money and that you would know what it was for," her mother's friend said.

Kelly's extended family has showered her with love and acceptance, giving her great peace about her father.

Kelly reunited with her brother

Debra Lewis formerly served as director of the Missing Persons Bureau in Chicago.

A Birthday Surprise

Reported by Ken Ramstead

"I'll never forget what you have done," wrote Liliane of Yarmouth, Nova Scotia. "Words alone cannot express my gratitude. It's a miracle."

That miracle was The Salvation Army's reuniting of Liliane with her long lost daughter, Lori. When Liliane and her husband separated, she returned to her native Canada from Germany, leaving Lori in his care. Liliane had not seen Lori since then, and the years apart had gradually eroded the mother–daughter bond. But the mother's sense of loss remained strong, and a friend finally contacted The Salvation Army in Canada. Canadian staff, in turn, notified the Army's office in Germany, and the search was underway.

A Worthwhile Wait

In short order, a caseworker tracked Liliane's daughter to Dusseldorf, Germany, and before long, she received the call she had been praying about for almost two decades.

"My long-lost daughter called me on my 35th birthday," Liliane said. "After the first shock of hearing her voice, tears of joy overcame me. It made the long wait worthwhile." The two quickly agreed to meet, and Lori flew to Canada.

"When I first saw my daughter, time stood still," said Liliane. Even though they had not seen one another in 19 years, it was as if they had never been apart, and those missing years simply disappeared. "How can one express in words the thoughtfulness of a friend and the work of The Salvation Army to make a lifetime dream come true?"

Ken Ramstead's story appeared in the Salvation Army publication, Faith & Friends, *in Canada.*

A Second Chance

Reported by the War Cry

Donna was born in West Germany to a poor family who already had two children. Her parents decided that they couldn't provide for a third child, and they gave Donna up for adoption.

A U.S. Army couple adopted her and the family moved to Arkansas, where Donna grew up. After her mother died and her father remarried, Donna began to look for her biological parents. She learned that her birth father was dead and that her birth mother had remarried. Her search seemed hopeless until she read in a Dear Abby newspaper column about The Salvation Army's program for reuniting families. Then she wrote to the Army's Missing Persons Bureau in Atlanta, GA, which contacted the Bureau in Germany. She discovered that her mother, Gertrud, had moved to Milan, Italy.

Gertrud, delighted to hear from Donna, arranged for her to visit her relatives in Europe, including two brothers and two sisters. One of Donna's brothers sent her money to cover her flight to Germany and drove her more than 2,000 miles throughout Europe to visit other family members.

"I want to thank you from the bottom of my heart for all you did to help me find my family," Donna wrote to The Salvation Army. "It worked out better than my greatest expectations. Now I have a second chance to have this new wonderful family. I'm overjoyed!"

"Call Me Collect"

Reported by The Salvation Army's Chicago Office

Darnell had raised her grandson, Eric, ever since he was a baby. Confident that he had grown up with good values, she still had some reservations about the woman he had married. Eric's new wife seemed to exert a bad influence on his ability to make decisions. After the couple moved to Florida, he'd stopped communicating with his grandmother.

Darnell asked The Salvation Army to find Eric, and some months later he was located, relieved to hear that his grandmother had been searching for him. His marriage had disintegrated, followed by a bitter divorce, and he had been left penniless. He'd also lost all of his personal belongings, had no way to contact his family, and had moved in temporarily with a friend. He contacted his grandmother right away, and she immediately wrote to thank the Missing Persons Bureau for finding him.

"I'm sending you a note that expresses my deepest gratitude for everything that you've done. My grandson and I talked on the telephone the other night. I'd written him and told him to call me collect. It was a blessing to hear his voice. It has lifted me in spirit and made me feel a lot better. Thank you and God bless you. Keep up the good work!"

Now They're Complete

Reported by The Salvation Army's Chicago Office

Meredythe walked out of the Salvation Army's Booth Hospital in Des Moines, IA, into a cold November day. Although her head told her she was taking the best course of action for her daughter, nothing could stop her heart from breaking.

Forty-five years later Kim began the search for her birth mother. Because her birth parents treated her openly and honestly, she had always known that she was adopted. After she contracted multiple sclerosis, Kim wanted more than ever to contact her birth mother and to learn her medical history.

She contacted the Booth Hospital Records Office, and The Salvation Army wrapped up the search in what seemed like record time. "I was excited because it happened so quickly," the caseworker said. "Meredythe called me back right away and I was able to get the two of them connected without any delays."

Meredythe, her husband and three children had been searching for Kim as well. Kim was overwhelmed to discover that her birth name was June Marie and that she had two half sisters and a half-brother.

Meredythe's family then arranged for Kim to attend a family reunion. While getting to know each other mother and daughter discovered that they even had jobs in the same field!

Meredythe and her daughter, Kim

Finding True Freedom

Reported by Douglas Peacock

Andrew wrote to The Salvation Army from prison to initiate a search for his mother, Connie, whom he hadn't seen in more than two decades. He had lost contact with her after his parents divorced, and his father was reluctant to provide any help. After another inmate told him about the Army's Missing Persons Bureau, he decided to fill out the standard questionnaire and hope for the best.

About a year later The Salvation Army located Connie. She'd tried to contact Andrew when he was a teenager, but she'd stopped searching after a friend of the family dissuaded her.

Once they connected, Connie, Andrew and his half-sister began to correspond. In December, he sent a Christmas card thanking the Army for finding his family, and for helping to bring about a Christmas celebration for them.

Connie also wrote: "I've been waiting 20 years to re-establish a relationship with my son. If not for your organization I'm sure I'd still be waiting. I finally got to see Andrew on Christmas Day. In sharing this story with other people, their reaction is similar to mine—they didn't know that The Salvation Army provided a missing persons service. It was a friend of my son's who told him about it." Connie enclosed a reunion picture of herself and Andrew.

"I Want To Know Him"

Reported by the War Cry

Tim was never allowed to see or correspond with his father after his parents went through a bitter divorce. Seeking the help of the Missing Persons Bureau in Chicago, he explained simply, "I want to know him. I have a son and I want him to know his grandfather. I pray every day that he would want to know me, my wife, and my son, Brandon."

The only lead Tim had was that his father had been a resident of Florida 10 years earlier. Armed with this small clue, the Bureau still managed to locate Leo in just three months. He responded with a long letter detailing the many attempts he had made to see his children after the divorce. He had finally halted his search after being dramatically chased away at gunpoint.

When Leo telephoned Tim, they talked for hours. That same month, Tim, his wife Sandy and their son traveled from Indiana to visit Leo in Florida. After 28 years, father and son were reunited in the sunshine state.

The reunion was a great success. Leo gave his newly found family a grand tour of the city and proudly introduced them to friends and neighbors. The whole family was eagerly anticipating a visit from Leo.

In a letter of thanks to The Salvation Army, Tim and Sandy wrote, "It couldn't have ended more happily for this family."

Loaves And Fishes

Reported by the War Cry

Cathi's brother Brian had disappeared off the face of the earth—or so it seemed to her family. Their last contact with him had been a Christmas card several years earlier.

Cathi and her family had tried every possible avenue to find Brian, with no success. She was especially concerned because their childhood home in Alaska had been torn apart by alcoholism, and she feared that he might be struggling with the same illness. She asked her friends to pray for him.

Years later Cathi's husband, Jim, a business administrator for The Salvation Army in Pasadena, CA, brought home an application from the Missing Persons Bureau. Even though Cathi was a Salvationist, she'd never thought of asking the Army for help. As she filled out the form, she despaired, because she had very little information about Brian, not even his social security number. The only possible lead was that he'd once spoken of moving to Florida. "There's a lot of ground between Alaska and Florida," she mused while mailing the completed form along with a nominal fee.

She was astonished to discover that her small contribution to the Army stretched further than the little boy's loaves and fishes in the New Testament parable. "Every eight weeks or so I'd receive a memo updating the Bureau's progress, which we found encouraging," she said.

Months passed, and most of the family lost hope. Finally, one evening the phone rang. "Sis?" a deep voice trembled. "Is Mom okay? This is Brian." He was alive and well and the family has remained in touch with him ever since.

Recognition

Reported by Debra Lewis

Fern's deepest desire had always been to reunite with her daughter Patricia, whom she had given up for adoption as a baby. Now that she lived in a nursing home with Alzheimer's disease, that hope seemed lost.

Patricia, meanwhile, had always wondered about her heritage and decided to seek her family's medical history from the Booth Records Office. After a Salvation Army caseworker located her brother David's address, the caseworker knew that her work was just beginning. A healthy mother-daughter connection could occur only through sensitive counsel and heartfelt prayer.

Many phone calls later, Patricia and her daughter, Jennifer, traveled to visit her mother. During a layover in Chicago, she received encouragement from the caseworker's words: "God still performs miracles, and when you see your mother, she'll know you." But when she reached her final destination, David warned her that Fern's disease had progressed to the point where she no longer recognized anyone.

Ultimately, faith won out. "Mama," she introduced herself, "I'm Patricia. I'm all grown up. I've found you and I've come to visit." Fern's face softened, and she enfolded Patricia in her arms. She also called David by name for the first time in several months. David felt certain that she understood that Patricia was her daughter. After the reunion, Patricia wrote to the Missing Persons Bureau, "I know in my heart that I've fulfilled Mama's dream . . . I'm at peace."

Patricia, Astrid (an Army caseworker), and Patricia's daughter Jennifer

Overwhelmed

Reported by Ruth Miller

Edith had moved to the West Coast, married, and then suffered a psychotic breakdown following the birth of her son. After her discharge from the hospital, she returned home to her husband and baby, but she had lost her ability to function. She couldn't cope, so she left behind a letter for them, along with her purse, keys, medication, and clothes, and then she simply disappeared.

Edith's four older sisters were all devastated by her disappearance. To make matters worse, her father was critically ill with a degenerative neurological disease.

Aside from emotional problems, Edith also struggled with diabetes, severe hypertension and high cholesterol. Her mother feared that she would not survive on the streets without money or medication to sustain her.

Desperate to find Edith, her mother wrote to The Salvation Army to initiate a search for her.

"If we didn't have a strong faith, we wouldn't have been able to stand the pain," her mother wrote. "If you hear from our daughter, please call us collect," she said. "All we want to know is that she is alive."

Six months later, after locating Edith, The Salvation Army received a grateful letter from her family. Her mother wrote that she had returned home, had found healing for some of her health problems, and possessed an "almost enviable" peace of mind. Edith and two of her sisters were planning a reunion with the rest of the family in Ohio.

The Laundromat

Reported by The Salvation Army's Chicago Office

Christopher, a native of Jamaica who struggled with paranoid schizophrenia, was missing, unemployed, and homeless. His ex-wife and children in the United States had no idea how to contact him. By way of The Salvation Army in France, his sister, Jaimee, initiated a search for him.

The Missing Persons Bureau obtained an address for him at a laundromat in Minneapolis, MN. After writing to him there, the staff received a phone call from the laundromat owner, who knew Christopher and had taken an interest in his welfare. He'd let him sleep at the laundromat off and on, had given him odd jobs to do, and had been trying to arrange housing for him.

Christopher often stopped by the laundromat and even had its phone number memorized. But lately, he hadn't been around much and he hadn't been spotted at any of his other usual hangouts.

After the laundromat owner talked to Jaimee, she sent Christopher two photos of their mother, which pleased him very much. The owner indicated that he would continue to try and find housing for him. Jaimee expressed profound gratitude that her brother was safe and that someone had been kind enough to offer him a helping hand.

The Peacemakers

Reported by Ruth Miller

The Salvation Army Missing Persons Bureau in West Nyack, NY received this letter of thanks for a job well done.

"May I say again how much we appreciate all of your efforts in locating our daughter. Although 18 years had passed with no word from her and you and I corresponded frequently, everything was negative. Suddenly, Voila!!! As we were vacationing for the winter, a letter arrived from our daughter Mary. It was a tentative letter, apologetic and slightly remorseful.

"She wrote that her husband had lost his parents six months apart and in his grief he said, 'I'd give anything if I had my parents back. You have parents and you don't seem to care.' This may have fueled her attempt to reconcile with us, although there was never any animosity on our part. I think as time went by it was more difficult for her. I understand.

"Now we are thrilled that we can meet another new son-in-law and enjoy two more grandchildren, to say nothing of embracing our long, lost daughter. Our anticipation is extreme. Our joy unimaginable! They are living on a 43-acre farm. Her husband has a master's degree and is now writing a book. Our daughter enjoys artwork, makes stained glass lampshades, and does organic gardening. We don't intend to be interrogators—the past is past. We'll listen to what she wants to tell us, but will spare her any recrimination."

"My Biggest Mistake"

Reported by The Salvation Army's Chicago Office

Marilyn had never forgotten her son Richard, who had been born 28 years earlier at the Booth Home and Hospital in Chicago. She had given him up for adoption, and, longing to connect with him, she sought assistance from Booth Hospital Records Office.

Marilyn drafted this letter to send to him: "In my heart I see you, pray for you, love you and regret the biggest mistake of my life—giving you up.

"Now, your brother and I have decided that we should try to find you. If you don't want to meet us, we'll understand and respect your wishes to be left alone. Until we meet, Godspeed and love always."

After six months, The Salvation Army located Richard, who had been renamed Darrin. He was living with a loving family, and his adoptive mother was delighted that Marilyn wanted to meet him. She understood that Darrin had a deep need to know his roots. The next three days he talked constantly by telephone with his new family. He learned that his birth mother, who was Sioux, lived on a reservation in South Dakota. His brother, Peter, bore a strong resemblance to him.

Marilyn, Peter and Darrin met in Chicago, where Darrin's adoptive mother welcomed them warmly into her home. They also visited The Salvation Army Missing Persons Bureau to meet the people who had brought about the reunion, sharing tears, joy and undying gratitude for God's mercy in their lives.

Crest Books

Salvation Army National Publications

Crest Books, a division of The Salvation Army's National Publications department, was established in 1997 so contemporary Salvationist voices could be captured and bound in enduring form for future generations, to serve as witnesses to the continuing mission of the Army.

Shaw Clifton, *Never the Same Again: Encouragement for New and Not–So–New Christians*, 1997

Compilation, *Christmas Through the Years: A War Cry Treasury*, 1997

William Francis, *Celebrate the Feasts of the Lord: The Christian Heritage of the Sacred Jewish Festivals*, 1998

Marlene Chase, *Pictures from the Word*, 1998

Joe Noland, *A Little Greatness*, 1998

Lyell M. Rader, *Romance & Dynamite: Essays on Science & the Nature of Faith*, 1998

Shaw Clifton, *Who Are These Salvationists? An Analysis for the 21st Century*, 1999

Compilation, *Easter Through the Years: A War Cry Treasury*, 1999

Terry Camsey, *Slightly Off Center! Growth Principles to Thaw Frozen Paradigms*, 2000

Philip Needham, *He Who Laughed First: Delighting in a Holy God* (in collaboration with Beacon Hill Press, Kansas City), 2000

Henry Gariepy, ed., *A Salvationist Treasury: 365 Devotional Meditations from the Classics to the Contemporary*, 2000

Marlene Chase, *Our God Comes: And Will Not Be Silent*, 2001

A. Kenneth Wilson, *Fractured Parables: And Other Tales to Lighten the Heart and Quicken the Spirit*, 2001

Carroll Ferguson Hunt, *If Two Shall Agree* (in collaboration with Beacon Hill Press, Kansas City), 2001

John C. Izzard, *Pen of Flame: The Life and Poetry of Catherine Baird*, 2002

Henry Gariepy, *Andy Miller: A Legend and a Legacy*, 2002

Compilation, *A Word in Season: A Collection of Short Stories*, 2002

R. David Rightmire, *Sanctified Sanity: The Life and Teaching of Samuel Logan Brengle*, 2003

Chick Yuill, *Leadership on the Axis of Change*, 2003

Compilation, *Living Portraits Speaking Still: A Collection of Bible Studies*, 2004

A. Kenneth Wilson, *The First Dysfunctional Family: A Modern Guide to the Book of Genesis*, 2004

Allen Satterlee, *Turning Points: How The Salvation Army Found a Different Path*, 2004

David Laeger, *Shadow and Substance: The Tabernacle of the Human Heart*, 2005

Check Yee, *Good Morning China*, 2005

Marlene Chase, *Beside Still Waters: Great Prayers of the Bible for Today*, 2005

Roger J. Green, *The Life & Ministry of William Booth* (in collaboration with Abingdon Press, Nashville), 2006

Norman H. Murdoch, *Soldiers of the Cross: Susie Swift and David Lamb, 2006*

Henry Gariepy, *Israel L. Gaither: Man with a Mission*, 2006

R.G. Moyles (ed.), *I Knew William Booth, 2007*

John Larsson, *Saying Yes to Life*, 2007

Frank Duracher, *Smoky Mountain High*, 2007

R.G. Moyles, *Come Join Our Army*, 2008

Ken Elliott, The Girl Who Invaded America: *The Odyssey of Eliza Shirley*, 2008

Ed Forster, *101 Everyday Sayings from the Bible*, 2008

Harry Williams, *An Army Needs An Ambulance Corps*, 2009

All titles by Crest Books can be purchased through your nearest Salvation Army Supplies and Purchasing department:

ATLANTA, GA—(800) 786–7372
DES PLAINES, IL—(800) 937–8896
LONG BEACH, CA—(800) 937–8896
WEST NYACK, NY—(888) 488–4882

Notes

Notes

Notes